George Henry Boughton, Amy M. Sacker, Mary Bowers Warren

Little Journeys Abroad

George Henry Boughton, Amy M. Sacker, Mary Bowers Warren

Little Journeys Abroad

ISBN/EAN: 9783744762168

Printed in Europe, USA, Canada, Australia, Japan

Cover: Foto ©Andreas Hilbeck / pixelio.de

More available books at **www.hansebooks.com**

LITTLE JOURNEYS ABROAD

BY

MARY BOWERS WARREN

With Original Illustrations by

GEORGE H. BOUGHTON, A.R.A.
E. K. JOHNSON, R.W.S.   IRVING R. WILES
J. A HOLZER   WILL H. DRAKE

BOSTON
JOSEPH KNIGHT COMPANY
1895

Dedicated

TO

MY FATHER

WITH WHOM I THUS ASSOCIATE

MY TRAVELS.

INTRODUCTION.

WITH so many books of travel in existence, it seems almost idle to add to their number. Travellers, however, seldom see things from the same point of view; and each new writer, with eyes open, discovers many an object of interest hitherto unnoticed.

The conventional book of travel is often a mere paraphrase of the guide-books, or commonplace description of the usual routine. Others are devoted to art, architecture, scenery, society, or politics, according as the fancy of the author dictates. So industriously and thoroughly has the field been gleaned that little is left for the late comer. Conscious of this, our author, passing over the subjects written upon by older and more experienced travellers, has chosen from the quiet by-ways of travel whither her valetudinarian fancy led her during a prolonged absence from home, those little episodes and experiences which add so much to the charm of Old-World life. These brief travel sketches, written out from memory, will, it is hoped, not only please and interest the untravelled reader, but also bring back pleasant memories to those who have been over the ground.

The interest in such a volume is always enhanced by illustrations, a generous supply of which have been here provided. In every instance they are from original drawings by well-known artists.

The cover design and other minor details of decoration were also specially made for the book.

With these few words of introduction the volume is offered to the favor of the public by

THE PUBLISHERS.

France.

	PAGE
THE FÊTE DIEU AND THE PARDON	1
MONT ST. MICHEL	20
PARISIAN PASTIMES	36

Germany.

A DAY IN SAXON SWITZERLAND	50
A VISIT TO CHIEM SEE	66
MUNICH AND FRANKFORT	78
AUTUMN DAYS IN NUREMBERG AND WEIMAR	90
HANOVER	105
IDLE MOMENTS IN GERMAN CAFÉS	127

Switzerland.

ON THE LAKE OF GENEVA	138
THE ESCALADE	151

Italy.

CERTOSA	160
A RAINY MORNING AT SAN MARCO	171
A WEDDING AT OUR PENSION	178

Algiers.

	PAGE
VILLA LIFE	187
DONKEYS AND CAMELS	206
AT THE JOHN BELL FOUNTAIN	217
INVALIDS, CHURCHES, AND CEMETERIES	232

England.

IN GOLF-LAND	250
WITH THE DONS IN OXFORD	274
IZAAK WALTON'S COUNTRY	294

·LIST OF ILLVSTRATIONS·

SUBJECT	ARTIST	PAGE
DESIGN FOR COVER	Amy M. Sacker.	
FRONTISPIECE	E. K. Johnson.	
HEADPIECE, CONTENTS	Amy M. Sacker	ix
HEADPIECE, LIST OF ILLUSTRATIONS	Amy M. Sacker	xi
CHOIR SCREEN, CATHEDRAL OF CHARTRES	J. A. Holzer	1
CHÂTEAU VILLEBON, CHARTRES	J. A. Holzer	5
CHÂTEAU MAINTENON, CHARTRES	J. A. Holzer	10
PEASANT, DINAN	George H. Boughton	11
PEASANT, FÊTE-DAY DRESS, DINAN	George H. Boughton	13
PEASANT, SUNDAY DRESS, DINAN	George H. Boughton	17
OUR LANDLADY	George H. Boughton	21
"WHITE-CAPPED DAMES SAT KNITTING"	George H. Boughton	25
MONT ST. MICHEL	J. A. Holzer	29
A PARISIENNE	Will H. Drake	36
TOWER OF ST. JACQUES	J. A. Holzer	43
ABBAYE DE SAINT-DENIS, SOUTH DOOR	J. A. Holzer	46
ZWINGERTHURM	J. A. Holzer	50
A GERMAN WAITING-MAID	E. K. Johnson	59

SUBJECT	ARTIST	PAGE
SCHLOSS HERRENCHIEMSEE, SAAL MIT DEM OCHSENAUGE	Will H. Drake	71
ISARTHOR, MUNICH	J. A. Holzer	78
GERMAN BEER-GARDEN	Will H. Drake	87
NASSAU HOUSE, NUREMBERG	J. A. Holzer	91
KAISERBURG, NEAR NUREMBERG	J. A. Holzer	95
GOETHE AND SCHILLER STATUE, WEIMAR	Will H. Drake	101
OLD CHURCH AND GOTHIC HOUSES, HANOVER	J. A. Holzer	111
CHARACTER HEAD, HANOVER	Will H. Drake	117
A GERMAN CAFÉ	Will H. Drake	125
A GERMAN WAITRESS	E. K. Johnson	129
GERMAN BEER-CELLAR	George H. Boughton	133
SWISS SAIL-BOAT	J. A. Holzer	138
ROUSSEAU'S ISLE	J. A. Holzer	145
SWISS GIRL	E. K. Johnson	153
OLD WELL, CERTOSA	J. A. Holzer	163
ITALY	George H. Boughton	169
SAVONAROLA'S CELL	J. A Holzer	173
FOUNTAIN OF NEPTUNE, BOBOLI GARDENS, FLORENCE	J. A. Holzer	178
PONTE VECCHIO, FLORENCE	J. A. Holzer	183
HEAD OF ARAB GIRL	George H. Boughton	187
STREET IN OLD ALGIERS	J. A. Holzer	193
ALGERIAN ARAB HEAD	Will H. Drake	199
DONKEY AND BOY	George H. Boughton	207
ALGERIAN ARABS AND CAMEL	Irving R. Wiles	213

LIST OF ILLUSTRATIONS. xiii

SUBJECT	ARTIST	PAGE
THE JOHN BELL FOUNTAIN	J. A. Holzer	217
ARAB AND DONKEY	Irving R. Wiles	223
ALGERIAN ARAB	Will H. Drake	227
GROVE NEAR ALGIERS	J. A. Holzer	232
MOSQUE, ALGIERS	J. A. Holzer	240
ARAB GENTLEMAN	Will H. Drake	243
ENGLISH COTTAGE	E. K. Johnson	251
AN ENGLISH GIRL	E. K. Johnson	257
RUSTIC MAIDEN	E. K. Johnson	261
GOLF-PLAYING	Will H. Drake	267
OXFORD AND CHERWELL RIVER	Will H. Drake	274
AN OXFORD DON	George H. Boughton	277
AN ENGLISH GIRL	E. K. Johnson	283
THE WORKER AND THE CRICKETER	George H. Boughton	289
HEADPIECE TO IZAAK WALTON'S COUNTRY	E. K. Johnson	294
UNEXPECTED VISITORS	E. K. Johnson	301
RURAL ENGLAND	E. K. Johnson	306
"AND I WILL NOT DENY BUT I THINK MYSELF A MASTER IN THIS"	Irving R. Wiles	311
TAILPIECE TO IZAAK WALTON'S COUNTRY	E. K. Johnson	313

CHOIR SCREEN, CATHEDRAL OF CHARTRES.

LITTLE JOURNEYS ABROAD.

THE FÊTE DIEU AND THE PARDON.

TRAVELLING through the pleasant country of France, we stayed over Sunday at Chartres, and found it to be a holiday of special interest on account of the celebration of the Fête Dieu,— a festival suppressed by the Revolution, and now, under the republic, no longer observed in Paris, and indeed only to be found in what we call in America the "rural districts." Quite fortunate we considered ourselves that morning, as we passed under the central portal of the west façade, surmounted by stiff, Byzantine figures of Christ and the Apostles, and entered the great, impressive cathedral.

Familiar with the interior from pictures, I was yet unprepared for the effect of majesty and vastness which burst upon us as we made our way under the massive arches, through a small number of worshippers, into the central aisle and very near the choir, where the choristers and clergy were already in their places. A number of brass instruments supplemented the organ, but the music was blatant and anything but pleasing. The choristers each wore a white cotta, tied by a red sash, and a red cape, edged with fur, and on their heads were wreaths of roses. The younger ones turned to form a circle around a portly personage, who beat time for the musicians; and the boys' earnest, wistful little faces, absorbed in their music, had something sweet and almost classic under their rose garlands,— even when there was an accompaniment of red hair and freckles.

High Mass was thus sung, the officiating priest and his assistants gorgeous in yellow vestments, stiff with embroidery and rich with jewels, and the altar decked with a wealth of roses. Preceded by the Swiss halberdiers, the procession filed out, passing great baskets of rose-leaves, ready for scattering in the procession through the streets later in the day. As they marched by, the thought came to my mind whether this feast of roses might not be a relic of some older festival kept by the ancient Druids, who had once held their services in the crypt in honor of the "Virgin who should bear a Child."

Musing thus, I strolled through the ambulatory, stopping to admire, on the wall enclosing the choir, the exquisite sculptures which tell the story of our Lord's life, and are worthy to be called a " Biblia Pauperum," so clear, strong, and natural every incident, so noble and graceful every figure, and so cunningly arranged the lace-like tracery beween the groups and the Gothic canopies and turrets above. One smiling Virgin bending over her smiling Babe haunts me as I write, so startling was its lifelikeness.

Passing on around the circuit of the seven chapels, finding something curious or interesting in each, I came suddenly on a little group of women kneeling with apparently greater devotion than anywhere else in the church, and directing their glances toward something in the obscure

CHÂTEAU VILLEBON, CHARTRES.

little chapel before them which I could not see. Coming nearer, I found the object of their worship to be the special treasure of the cathedral, Our Lady of the Pillar, a dark wooden figure of a Madonna and Child, dating from the fifteenth century. The faces of both Mother and Child are quite black, and form a curious contrast to the white satin, gold-embroidered robes in which they are dressed. The marble pillar on which the image rests is kissed with great reverence by the pilgrims, who approach it kneeling; and above the head and to the right and left on the walls of the chapel, were thousands of little votive hearts of gold and silver, making a rich background for the dark little figure that has been so venerated for four hundred years. There were hanging lamps burning here, and a great candelabrum full of lighted candles, and crowds pressing around continually; but my companion was beckoning me, and I hastened on, for we had to return to our hotel *déjeûner* before coming out to see the procession.

Punctually at three the procession started from the cathedral, at its head a number of little girls dressed in white, singing, and scattering rose leaves, and wearing wreaths of roses. Their hair was curled with an elaborateness that told of many an hour in curl-papers, and reminded us of the glimpses we had caught the day before through the windows of the hairdressers' shops, and which we had called little genre pictures, not unlike the pictures of Dow and Van Mieris, before which we had so often lingered in the galleries. Fat, commonplace-looking Sisters marshalled the children on their way, and made place for the next detachment of the procession. Numbers of young girls in blue dresses and white veils, carrying rich banners, many more in the white "first communion" dress, were followed by long lines of Sisters, priests, and widows in little close white caps. Finally came the choristers, swinging censers, scattering rose leaves, chanting and turning ever and anon to bow and genuflect with military precision before the Host, which was carried under a golden canopy by a superbly vested, white-haired priest, surrounded by others in purple and yellow damask furred robes. Unfortunately, the meaning of this magnificence of apparel was all unknown to us, and we longed for some Roman Catholic friend to explain it. The procession passed on its way up and down the hilly streets of Chartres, and we hastened down one particularly steep and uncomfortably stony hill to an open square. Here a temporary altar had been erected, decked with a beautifully embroidered cloth, and banked with roses; while on either side were massed hundreds of potted plants,—geraniums, roses, and hydrangeas.

After a weary time of waiting, we were rewarded by the arrival of the advance

CHÂTEAU MAINTENON, CHARTRES.

guard of peasants, followed by choristers and priests; a short and solemn service was chanted, and once more the procession melted away down the hill on its way to another altar. Thoughtfully we returned

THE FÊTE DIEU AND THE PARDON. 11

to our hotel, picking up on our way some of the roses which were lying on the road.

The next Sunday found us at Dinan in time for the Dinan celebration of the Fête Dieu; and the procession, though smaller, was much the same in character, although of course the rich vestments and altar services were lacking. Two little children headed the long line of singing boys; one in a pink satin frock, leading a lamb, represented the infant Saint John, while the other carried a cross as the emblem of the infant Saviour. The peasants had hung sheets on the walls of the houses, and decorated them with garlands of roses; and the effect at a distance was really somewhat that of the old satin and brocaded hangings that draped the build-

PEASANT, DINAN.

ings for gala occasions in feudal days. Pleased with all we had seen, we decided to go on Monday to Guingamp for a couple of days, to see something of the Pardon there.

The journey was somewhat tedious and uninteresting; but once arrived in the crowd of variously costumed peasants, and established in the quaint inn, not far from the festively decorated mediæval church, we were well content that we had come. A journey among the booths, the merry-go-rounds, and to the horse and cattle market, showed us so many old people, and so many sad faces, that we asked the landlady where were the young people, the music and dancing. The young people, she explained, held their Pardon in the autumn, and there were lively times then; but this was more for the older people, and there were church services and hymn-singing instead of dancing. Accor-

PEASANT, FÊTE-DAY DRESS, DINAN.

dingly, we went the next morning to the service in the church, and heard an address from a foreign and long-bearded bishop, commending the people of Guingamp and the neighboring country on their observance of old customs. He was a missionary bishop, and told several anecdotes illustrating the fact that he found his previous knowledge of medicine highly useful among the people for whose spiritual welfare he now labored. But he must have felt that medical knowledge was scarcely needed at Guingamp, when he looked at the rows of hardy, rosy old faces before him, that spoke eloquently of years of hard work and robust health. Eight thousand devout souls gathered there to receive absolution of sins, to make thank-offerings for mercies received, and offer votive gifts and prayers for blessings on flocks and fields, and for a bountiful harvest.

That afternoon there was a brisk sale of candles; and by eight o'clock in the evening, the illuminations of tiny colored lamps strung across the street, forming the letters of Ave Maria, were all ablaze, and every one was crowding to the church for the final service, and to light his or her candle at a church candelabrum. We, too, followed and bought our candles from a smiling old woman at the door, and lighted them from one held by a bewildered peasant near by. We did not join in the procession, as did two young English boys, who seemed to enter it from a spirit of fun, and to become more and more impressed by the solemnity of the scene as they trudged along; still, we watched with breathless interest its departure and its return. Touched anew by the plaintive singing, the glimmering of the candles in the darkness, the sight of the statues carried by the school-boys and

SUNDAY DRESS, DINAN.

school-girls, we made our way back to the old inn. The stalwart priests, the lame in wheeled chairs, the crowd of peasants, with here and there a richly dressed lady in their midst, passed slowly by, and the pageant melted away into darkness.

MONT ST. MICHEL.

WE arrived at Mont St. Michel on a bright afternoon, and, engaging one of the little carriages waiting at the station, started on our drive over the causeway and up the steep hill to the hotel of Madame P. the elder. There was a rival hotel kept also by a Madame P., a sister-in-law of the elder one, and where also a sign above the door informed one of the excellence of the omelettes made there; but we had been warned by a friend to intrust ourselves only to the ancient, the *véritable*, the beautiful Madame P., and, if possible, to secure rooms in the *dépendance* farther up the hill. So we had written and received a favorable answer, and felt quite sure of our welcome. A sudden shower had obscured our view of the mount and castle as we drove upward; and it was from behind the drawn curtains of the carriage that we peered out, to see at the door the handsome face of Madame P. She assured us that our rooms were ready at the *dépendance*, and also, as we glanced at the fire on the great hearth, that we should surely see her make an omelette there before we left. This we knew to be a sight almost equal in importance to the castle.

OUR LANDLADY.

So we contentedly climbed up the many steps to the building where we were to be located, and after a short time of resting, ventured out for a turn on the ramparts. We had scarcely taken ten steps, and were leaning over the wall to look at a curious little vegetable-garden on the rocks below, when suddenly we were importuned by a pretty young girl; then a second, even prettier, and finally a third from the steps above, joined in urging, entreating, advising the ladies in the best possible English to visit the Musée. What was it? It might be interesting, and we had an hour or two to while away. So we weakly yielded, purchased our tickets, and entered the Musée. It was so dark that we stumbled and gave a little cry of horror.

"Do not be afraid," said the little girl; "I will go with you;" and she took my hand in hers. But we did not quite enjoy

the picture before us of wax figures in
armor, representing the combat of the
French and English on the sands, when
the invading English were finally over-
whelmed in the flood. The next picture
was somewhat better: Gautier, the sculptor, working in his cell. Yet he, too, was
much too lifelike for our taste, and we
turned with pleasure to see the pretty,
flaxen-haired figure of Du Guesclin's
young wife, leaning from the window of
the house to which he had committed her
for safety, to point to him a happy presage
of future victory in the stars that shone in
the skies of those troublous times. Yes,
our sympathy and sentiment were touched
at this; but at sight of the unfortunate
Cardinal Balue, gnawed by rats in the iron
cage where he was thrown by the cruel
order of Louis XI., we turned and fled,
escaping from the entreaties of our little
guide, and hastened with closed eyes past

the horrid figures, back to the welcome light of day, fresh air, and the sunset quiet of the ramparts.

White-capped old dames sat knitting at the doors of the tiny stone houses built along the ramparts, where probably soldiers and sentries had formerly lived, and each old lady wished us "bon soir!" as we passed. One or two men in blue blouses passed us, giving us a steady look of scrutiny from dark eyes, and bowing as they rattled their tools or swung a string of fish. On the sands below us were two or three bare-legged women gathering shells. Pools and channels of rivers filtered through the sands, and beyond us rolled the tossing waves of the bay. We could see in the distance the outlines of Avranches; and we experienced that calm feeling of rest and shelter that one has on an island cut off from the excitement of the outer world.

"WHITE-CAPPED DAMES SAT KNITTING."

On the rock above us was the little house pointed out as being the very one, at least in part, in which the Constable Bertrand du Guesclin left his young wife during his absence in time of war. Mont St. Michel had always been a fortified stronghold, for six hundred men from here joined William the Norman in his expedition against England; and in 1361 the castle, no trace of which now remains, was intrusted by Charles the Wise to Du Guesclin, to hold as a frontier post against the English. During his absence on a foraging expedition, it suffered and repulsed an attack of the English, who were aided by the plots of an English prisoner, Felton, with the waiting-maids of young Madame du Guesclin.

All the country through which we had been travelling was filled with the name and fame of the great Constable, so that we were now familiar with the life and deeds of the Breton hero of the Middle Ages. And for the encouragement of mothers of unruly boys, let me record that a contemporary chronicle states that he was "the ugliest child from Rennes to Dinan, flat-nosed and swarthy, thickset, broad-shouldered, big-headed, a bad fellow, a regular wretch, according to his own mother's words, given to violence, always striking or being struck, whom his tutor abandoned without having been able to teach him to read." These fighting propensities were doubtless prophetic of the future career of the great warrior; but his stern character was tempered by honesty, justice, and modesty, for he tried to excuse himself from assuming the office of constable, saying, "Dear sir and noble King, I do pray you to have me excused; I am a poor knight and petty bachelor." But the King would listen to no excuse, and delighted in giving, "together with the office,

MONT ST. MICHEL.

many handsome and great estates for himself and his heirs." Touching is the story of his dying at the age of sixty-six before Châteauneuf-de-Randon, a place that he was besieging, and with his last words exhorting the captains round him "never to forget that, in whatsoever country they might be making war, churchmen, women, children, and the poor were not their enemies;" and the coming of the governor to his bier, saying he would surrender to no other than Du Guesclin, and laying the keys at the feet of the dead. The Constable was buried at St. Denis, and the Bishop of Auxerre delivered the funeral oration. According to a poet of the time —

> "The tears of princes fell,
> What time the bishop said,
> 'Sir Bertrand loved ye well;
> Weep, warriors, for the dead!'
> The knell of sorrow tolls
> For deeds that were so bright:
> God save all Christian souls
> And his — the gallant knight!"

We lingered over the Breton story; and the next morning, as we climbed the grass-grown flights of stairs, hanging to the side of the rock, and with a small party of tourists passed under the turreted baronial gateway, we talked of the romantic history of the pile before us, the Pagan priests who had first inhabited the wild Mount, the Druid sacrifices, the milder Christian monks who succeeded them, the Norman dukes and kings who built the church and the fortress. Thousands of pilgrims once yearly visited the shrine, and here the royal devotees prostrated themselves as penitents. In the memorable war when Henry V. of England won the battle of Agincourt, and conquered nearly all France to boot, Mont St. Michel was preserved to the French, as Calais was preserved to the English. What a realistic picture of the Middle Ages this all grew to be, as we dwelt upon the miseries and secrets of the oubliettes, the rigors of the iron cage, and the story of the escape of the quick-witted prisoner by means of the machinery with which the monks raised their provisions for the winter!

Many are the stories of heroism and endurance which cluster about this most romantic structure, and in its presence the imagination finds free scope.

Rich and powerful the abbey must have been with its dependencies, one of which was St. Michael's Mount in Cornwall, and its influence must have gone out abroad, and its name been honored far beyond the confines of the ancient realm of France. The guide droned out his stories as we followed through the dark and deserted halls of the granite convent building. The Merveille, as it is called, consists of three stories, the lower one a series of vaulted crypts; above this two noble halls, and above all, the beautiful cloisters and dormitory. Mutilated and ruinous was the greater part of the building; but the noble proportions of the chamber of knights, where were held the chapters of the knights of the Order of St. Michel, founded by Louis XI. in 1496, rewarded one for the rough climbing and the pushing through narrow doorways and corridors. Leaving the graceful creations of foliage, sprigs, flowers, and garlands, executed with wonderful variety of design on the spandrils of the arches of the cloisters, we came out on a grass-grown space in the open air, where I suppose the monks used to take their exercise. One of the tourists — a Frenchman who had evidently been bored by the guide's anecdotes, and had tried to frighten the ladies of his party in the prisons — here sang and laughed at escaping from the dreary interior, and even indulged in mild badinage with the guide who had just described to us the semi-Romanesque, semi-Gothic carvings of Scriptural subjects in the church.

A wondrous pile, both craggy rock and castle church, wondrous in historic associations, grand in natural beauties, stately in the dignity of art, and sacred forever, will it be in the memory of two Americans who visited it that day.

PARISIAN PASTIMES.

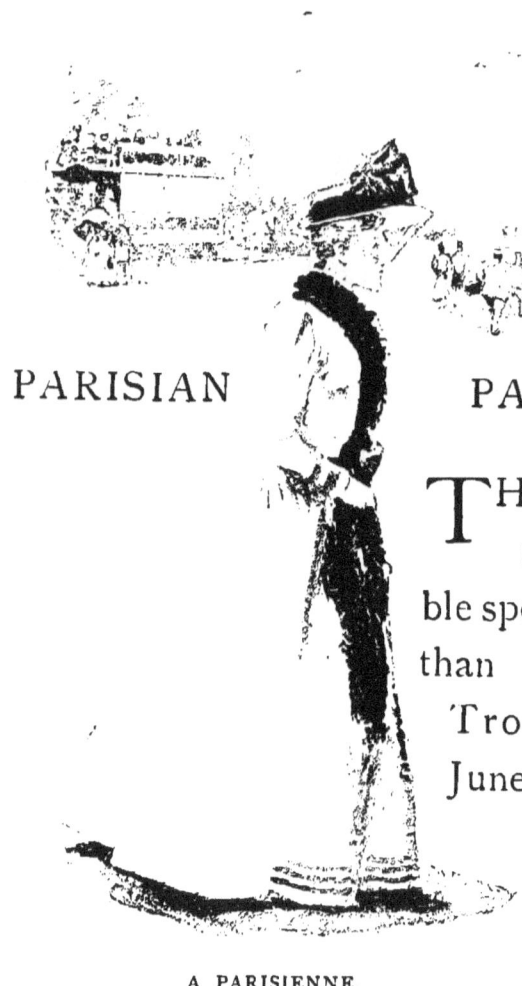

A PARISIENNE.

THERE is no more agreeable spot to be found than the Avenue Trocadéro in June, when the chestnut-trees are in bloom, and carriages are continually passing on the way to the Bois de Boulogne, and riders are trotting by on the bridle-road in the centre of the street, and the Moorish outlines of the Trocadéro Palace, and the spider-like ones of the Eiffel Tower are outlined clearly against the sky.

It was sufficient for us to see those spider-like outlines, however, for we felt no airy aspirations, and were content to allow our friends to journey skyward, while we took our way on foot to the Trocadéro Park, and continued on to the Bois. It was cool and pleasant, for we were on high ground, and near the Seine; and we enjoyed returning to the wide avenue and pure air after excursions dutifully undertaken to the Louvre and the old quarters of Paris. Until 1866, said our guide-book, this land was nothing but a piece of waste ground, although Napoleon I. had once entertained the idea of building a marble palace here for the King of Rome. But in 1867 the undulating ground was laid out in terraces, and used as a place for popular festivals, and for the exhibition of 1878 the present palace was constructed.

With our friends in the *pension* we were a party of five,— the "five lively ladies," we were called; and one of the five discovered that there were various attractions down the Champs Elysées in the afternoons for those who were frivolously inclined, or who were debarred by nervous prostration from undertaking very arduous sight-seeing.

Therefore down the Champs Elysées we all strolled one afternoon, making our way through throngs of people on our search for — what do you think?— Guignol and *gouffres au lait.* A steady stream of people was pouring up toward the Arc de Triomphe; but the children and their *bonnes* lingered about the spot whither our steps were turning. There was the little puppet stand; there was the row of benches, a few children already in their places; there was the musician playing a doleful accordion; and there was Madame la Propriétaire, a portly figure, looking out smilingly to attract an audience, and nodding encouragingly to us.

But not a little was our embarrassment to discover across the way another Guignol, — a Guignol equally importunate, for we could hear his shrill tones, as the farce had already begun; a Guignol housed in a structure equally gorgeous in red, blue and yellow paint; a Guignol heralded by a fife instead of an accordion — still a Guignol whose proprietor was a man! *Va pour le Guignol feminin!* A broad smile on the part of Madame rewarded us when she saw that we had decided to "assist" at her entertainment; and behold us then seated on one of the front benches, dropping centimes into the cap of the musician, who takes this opportunity before the rising of the curtain, and shaking from our dresses the blossoms that fell from the chestnut-tree, which formed, with its leafy branches, a canopy over our heads.

The curtain rose, with again the sound of music, and the play began,— a play whose every point of delicious humor was appreciated as never yet were the *jeux d'esprit* at the Théâtre Français. We perhaps formed the claque, for we applauded without stint, and encouraged the laughing French children around us to do the same; and at the applause, clap, clap, the blows rained harder than ever on poor little Guignol, and the policeman mercilessly rapped his head against the floor.

The play concerned itself chiefly, as we made out, with the misfortunes of a mischievous baker's boy on a certain New Year's day, who delivers rolls to the wrong persons, disobeys his master, and commits many *mauvaises plaisanteries* in the course of one day of his vicious career. For Guignol must surely have ended with the guillotine if he continued in his evil ways. Compared with the English Punch, he was more tricky, more refined, more amusing, we thought, and — there was no wife-beating; our sex was respected. *Encore une fois va pour le Guignol feminin!* It was the ten centimes fee, we concluded, though my companion, whose acquaintance with the French language was of recent date, was somewhat puzzled over the jokes — would I could remember that exquisite one on the old gentleman's *souliers!* — and thought that Guignol's accent was none of the purest. We were very particular as to accents in those days.

The dispersing audience of children melted away toward the merry-go-rounds, the weighing machines, and the booths where you were photographed on the spot, and instantaneously; but we turned to the pagoda, where the sign assured us that we could eat *gouffres au lait*, and drink syrups of every color and flavor. The proprietor was a large, dignified man with a benign expression, and he too smiled on us in a fatherly way when, at my companion's adjuration to "talk French at him," I did talk French at him in a way that surprised him, I am sure. Yet he understood, however erratic my grammar may have been, and opened the door in the flooring, and, descending to his *cave*, produced his choicest *groseille*, and fell to work making what we considered crisp, brown, delicious *gouffres au lait*, which, powdered with white sugar, we consumed in a manner that completely satisfied him as to our appreciation. How immaculate were his cap and apron, and how spotlessly clean every inch of his domain! We, at least, were so pleased with our repast that we induced an Eng-

TOWER OF ST. JACQUES.

lish gentleman at the *pension* to meet us on the Champs Elysées another afternoon for a second " waffling " party; but whether he objected to the powdered sugar that was brushed perforce over his face, or whether the English masculine thirst craves something stronger than *groseille*, we became painfully aware that he did not share our enthusiasm as to the superlative delicacy of the *gouffres au lait*.

We had spent several afternoons in the mediæval rooms of the Musée de Cluny, and becoming enthusiastic over the things of the Middle Ages, voted for a visit to the Sainte-Chapelle. A long journey it was from the Avenue Trocadéro, and necessitated changes in the omnibuses; and the little gem of Gothic architecture was almost hidden by the surrounding buildings when we reached it, so that we did not realize the beauties of the palace-chapel of Louis the Good, the Crusader King of France, until we

ABBAYE DE SAINT-DENIS, SOUTH DOOR.

had entered the building. We did not linger long among the tombs of canons once attached to the chapel, but followed a party of four French sisters up the spiral staircase to the upper chapel. Here, falling into a revery, I was transported in spirit, as I had been in the Hotel Cluny, back to feudal days, and could see the pious King on his knees in rapt devotion before the sacred relics which he had purchased from the King of Jerusalem and the Emperor of Constantinople, and for the reception of which he built this chapel. The altar and the Gothic canopy now only mark the spot where the relics were formerly preserved; but part of the glass in the beautiful windows which picture the lives of saints, and also one of the small gilded spiral staircases, date from the time of Saint Louis. The pillars, the statues of the Apostles, the gilding and decoration of the walls, though partly restored, — all breathed of the past, and carried us from the age of electricity, materialism, and critical analysis to the age of Faith and Love.

That evening we had a box at the Théâtre Français, suggesting the seventeenth century and the time of Molière. Unfortunately, we thought, no play of Molière's was given at that time, but instead one of the younger Dumas's lighter and amusing comedies; and, sitting with our feet snugly ensconced on "petits bancs," we enjoyed the wit of the dialogue, the finished graceful acting of the performers, and, thanks to our two English escorts, who laboriously studied the playbook, were able to follow the plot. In the interlude arrived pretty little pink ices, after tasting which, we strolled through the *foyer* and corridors, where are statues of Talma, Voltaire, Rachel, and George Sand. The floor of the corridor was slippery, and invited the younger members of the party to a prolonged slide; and as that particular corridor was absolutely deserted at that moment, one by one, the members of the party joined in the exercise, and found that, if a little undignified, it was a grateful relief from the long sitting and listening to a play in a foreign tongue. A merry drive home in the rain, our hats handkerchief-covered, for the cabs were open ones, completed our evening.

A DAY IN SAXON SWITZERLAND.

ZWINGERTHURM.

A PERFECT day in June, and in Dresden so perfect that my friend Egeria and I decided to make an excursion into the picturesque country near us, which is called Saxon Switzerland. Our objective point was the Bastei. The southern part of the kingdom of Saxony, beginning about eight miles above Dresden and extending beyond the Bohemian frontier, from its mountainous character is called Saxon Switzerland, although it has none of the snow-peaks, glaciers, or massive grandeur of real Swiss scenery.

The river Elbe flows through the centre of this country; and the mountains of the Giant, the Riesengebirge, and the Erzgebirge form the boundary between it and Bohemia. Among these rocks are found beds of jet, kaolin, fuller's earth, marble, slate, agate, jasper, and chalcedony, and the Saxon silver mines are as celebrated as Saxony woollens. The Bastei, or Bastion, is the name given to one of the largest masses of rock which rise on the right bank of the river. Great blocks of calcareous sandstone form a wall, through which narrow lanes and gorges are cut, as though by some effort of modern engineering.

The action of water is everywhere visible, as the rocks are never angular, but smoothly rounded, rising in pyramids and pillars, tapering in a conical form to dilate again as they rise higher, resembling on a large scale those cavern formations where a descending stalactite rests on an ascending stalagmite.

The sandstone crumbles down into a soil soft to the feet, making easy walking for the pedestrian. To the lover of romance and legend, this district is specially attractive, for it is the country of Saxon and Bohemian gnomes, kobolds, and good and evil spirits of every denomination. In the gloomy recesses of the Lilienstein, whose summit is nine hundred feet above the level of the river, the simple peasant folk still locate fairy guardians of hidden treasure; and somewhere among the caverns of the Nonnenstein weeps and prays the holy nun who was miraculously transported thither from a lapsed community, while the Maiden's Leap perpetuates, in name, the Saxon maid who threw herself from its precipice to evade her pursuers.

Whether the Scops, or wandering singers of South Saxony in England, as Sussex was then called, wove into their Christian ballads the tricksy spirits of their native fastnesses in the guise of demons to be conquered by knightly gentleness, and whether their harps sounded with an errant sweetness, smothered by echoes of the winds that swept through these wilds in fairy times, we know not, but we may conjecture that some of the heroes and deities exiled by Saint Wilfrid's preaching returned again to take dominion of their German rocks.

So, having determined to venture into this land of magic, which did not seem unlike our own Catskill country, we left our *pension* at eight o'clock in the morning, and after carefully selecting the bluest and therefore the best *droschky* on the stand, drove off amid a shower of good wishes from Frau von B. and her three daughters.

I might here remark that we had been studying German, but, alas! after four weeks' daily intercourse with a German family, had acquired only a bewildering knowledge of that bewildering language, and still found difficulty in making ourselves understood. We were amused by seeing in a window a notice in English, " Languages and Knowledges taught here." Although we had come to Europe chiefly for the sake of acquiring " knowledges," we concluded that we felt unable just at the outset to grapple with so vast a subject, and therefore contented ourselves with our one language and a few lectures on the history of art in connection with the Dresden picture-gallery.

Fortunately, our driver understood our feeble German, and brought us in good season to our boat, the " Germania," which stood waiting at the wharf, below the fashionable promenade of the Bruhlsche

Terrace. As we sailed up the Elbe, we looked back at the fine domes of the Frauenkirche and the Royal Catholic Church (for although the greater part of his subjects are Protestants, the king adheres to the Roman Church), the clock tower of the old palace, the graceful arches of the Augustus Bridge, and the turreted front of the great barracks.

There were few passengers, and we glided rapidly along the narrow, winding river, glistening in the sunlight; past Loschwitz, where is seen, in the midst of a vineyard near the road, the small house where Schiller wrote the greater part of his "Don Carlos," working there in the early morning in view of the river. Farther up the river, we came to Hosterwitz, where Von Weber composed the opera of "Der Freischütz," and Pillnitz, — the royal Japanese villa directly on the water's edge, toward which the carriage with the royal liveries was crossing on the ferry. On either hand were hillsides with vines and old towers, and sunny slopes where women were making hay; or peaceful villages and dwellings, in whose red-tiled roofs the "eye" windows looked inquisitively at us. Passing Pirna, and not forgetting that here in the Dominican convent once lived Luther's old antagonist, the monk Tetzel, we came to our stopping-place, Wehlen, where we landed. We were the only tourists, and all the guides and various idlers waiting at the wharf followed us to a cluster of blocks of stone, where, with some trepidation, we mounted our horses, and, led by the guides, started on our first equestrian excursion. The road led at once into the pine forest, and we began the ascent, which was, after all, quite easy, and wound upward along the ravine of Uttewaldergrund. The road became very narrow; the branches met overhead;

and between the leaves we caught glimpses of solid walls of rock towering above us, and of deep grewsome caves where Siegfried's dragon might have lain hid.

Indeed, so romantic grew the scene around us that we would not have been surprised to meet Siegfried, good sword in hand, at any turn of the road; or on one of the isolated peaks to see Brünhilde stand while the magic flames leaped around the base. And the birds sang the same songs, and the echoes repeated the same notes of the horn, which we had heard in Wagner's opera the evening before.

It was all so fairy-like that we did not like to break the charm by conversation; and of our guides, the young one was too shy to talk, and the old one was too much occupied in brushing away the flies which sadly troubled our horses. But we duly noticed the turrets, tables, castles, stone houses, and devil's kitchen among the marvellous sandstone formations on our left in the ravine, and, glancing upward, wondered at the tall pines springing from crevices in the rock high above us.

As we neared the summit, there was a wonderful stone bear, crouched high above us, turning his head to look at the Bastei. Here we passed a gay picnic party, encamped on the roadside. They looked at us with interest, and seemed to find something amusing in our appearance. Can it be possible that we looked unused to the saddle? We emerged quite suddenly and unexpectedly, and found a scene full of life. The usual German restaurant awaited us; and at little tables sat happy people eating and drinking, and — no, for once not knitting and crocheting, but fully enjoying the prospect, and raving as Germans always do, over the beautiful *Aussicht.* We ate our dinner very contentedly, hav-

A GERMAN WAITING-MAID.

ing found real English roast beef, and then wandered about, seeking the different points of view.

From the narrow block on the summit of the Bastei, we looked for miles over the amphitheatre of the surrounding country seven hundred feet below us. The Elbe wound sleepily below, looking very different from the same busy river at Dresden. On the right bank lay the village of Nieder-Rathen, and opposite us was Ober-Rathen and the ruins of an ancient castle. Beyond rose the mound of the Königstein, a virgin fortress, almost the only one in Europe never yet taken by force. In time of war the works of art, picture-gallery, and Green Vault treasures of Saxony, have always been preserved in this fortress; and Frederick Augustus II. himself took refuge here during the Seven Years' War. It is so far removed from any other height that it cannot be commanded by artillery,

Napoleon having tried in vain to batter it from the Lilienstein. The approach, through a slanting way cut in the living rock, and the outworks and drawbridges, are said to give it the appearance of the hill-forts in India. Between Königstein and the Lilienstein was the round top of the Pfaffenstein, and in the distance green hills and valleys, and a small steamboat slowly disappearing around a curve in the river, — altogether, a peaceful scene in the afternoon sunlight.

As we stood there, we heard fresh young voices singing; and presently came the tramp of many feet, and we were besieged by an army of school-boys, led by a burly teacher, and having each one the inevitable oblong green tin botanical case slung across his shoulder. Ousted from our point of vantage, we tried the Wehlenstein, only to be driven from our contemplation of the quaint, rocky monsters by a club of young men; and so, after admiring the stone bridge built across a large chasm in 1878, under the auspices of King Frederick Augustus, and noticing the inscription to the memory of the two worthy and adventurous clergymen, Nicolai and Gotzinger, who discovered this region one hundred years ago, we turned to descend.

This time it was *zu Fuss*, and we were glad, as we slipped and stumbled over the pine needles and clambered down the stone steps, stopping often to rest and to inquire our way of the women selling glasses, laces, and pictured post-cards in the occasional little booths along the road. Siegfried was still in our thoughts as we continued our way through the lovely but quieter scenery of the Amselgrund down to Rathen. The road lay along a deep stream; and near the bank were more women making hay, while a sunburned farmer looked calmly on. Although ever righteously indignant about the downtrodden women of Germany, I noticed that on that day Egeria had not a word to say of woman's rights, as her picture-loving eye rested on the figures in the field.

At Rathen we were to find the ferry to take us across the Elbe to Ober-Rathen, whence we were to be returned by rail to Dresden. Two other ladies and a little girl were waiting for the ferry, and the old ferryman sculled us over, grumbling somewhat at the small number of tourists, but withal, bidding us adieu civilly, as every one did, and standing to watch us as we made our way to the station. After a very hot, uncomfortable journey, we reached Dresden. Our return was much earlier than we had expected, and we found the Von B's had taken advantage of our absence to give a tea-party to their friends under the cherry-trees in the garden. But we did not wait long, for our good friend, rosy-cheeked Anna, brought us a tray with our *Abendessen*, and with it, strawberries and *Süsskuchen* from the party. So — a truly German "so!" of contentment — we had spent a happy day in Saxon Switzerland.

A VISIT TO CHIEM SEE.

IN the Alpine region in Southern Bavaria lies the Chiem See, on the shore of which the unfortunate Louis II. built one of his most beautiful palaces. While we were in Munich, we became interested in the romantic history of that monarch, and our interest led us to Chiem See.

Although the day was Friday, and one of ill omen in the eyes of our superstitious landlady, and she was vehement in her assertions that we would find the palace closed, still as the sun shone brightly, we rose early and took the train, a party of eleven ladies, at half-past eight. After a journey of an hour and a half through a pleasant country, we changed to an odd little steam tram for half an hour more to

Prien, then another half hour across the lake, and we had reached our destination.

Chiem See is the largest lake in Bavaria, and is very picturesque, containing three islands, — Herreninsel, Fraueninsel, and Krautinsel. The last is a tiny islet which lies between Fraueninsel and the larger Herreninsel, on which the castle is built. We followed the path through the wood in view of the lake and past the old Schloss Herrenwörth. This is a pile of yellow buildings, simple in design, and was formerly a Benedictine convent, founded by Duke Thassilo in the days when the whole island was owned by the Benedictine order.

During 1881, King Louis lived in this old castle while superintending the building of the new one, but during the last two years he lived in the finished apartments of the new palace. The story is told that every evening he caused the whole building to be illuminated, and the five thousand candles in the *Spiegelgallerie* to blaze brightly in the thousand mirrors, while he strolled alone back and forth over the long expanse of polished floor.

During the building, a track had been laid from the castle to the lake for the *Rollwagen*, which carried up the stone and other material for building. Louis caused a *Rollwagen* to be draped with tapestry and a gilded *fauteuil* from the castle placed on it. Seated in this, and wearing his fantastic Lohengrin dress and silver armor, he journeyed to the shore on moonlight midnights to be rowed on the lake in a gilded gondola; into such vagaries did his splendor-loving fancy lead him.

We, who had seen, in the royal stables in Munich, his gorgeous gilded coaches and sleighs, could well imagine the scene.

Remembering the fairy-like sleigh, surmounted by a pyramid of gold Cupids bearing stars of electric light, no tale of whimsical splendor seemed extravagant. Enveloped in cushions and robes of pale blue velvet and white fur, with a footman standing in the velvet shoes at the back of this sleigh, the handsome, yet sad-faced Louis was wont in winter to dash through the streets of his capital. It is said that he gave as a reward to the engine-master, who propelled the *Rollwagen* by an engine used in the water-works, a gold watch adorned by an exquisite miniature of himself.

Gold, gold, gold! he could brook no meaner metal; and it seemed as if, Midas-like, all that those long, white fingers touched became golden, and wherever those melancholy eyes rested, there flashed back a glow of aureate splendor. And the very earth of his kingdom grew golden according to his desire, for the mines of Bavaria gave rich yields of ore. This magnificent palace before us was only one of the many he built.

Entertained by these stories and reminiscences, we had reached, and paused to admire, the great fountains in front of the castle. Here are bronze groups, — one Pegasus, the other Fortuna, standing on her wheel; but the great basins are now filled in with earth and grass-covered, as the water-works, which cost originally half a million marks, have been taken out and sold.

The middle building — Mittelbau — is one hundred and two metres long, and the façade is adorned by statues. Entering the hall, we were confronted by a noble bronze and silver enamelled peacock with drooping tail, who looked majestically down on his timid helpmeet crouching at his feet.

SCHLOSS HERRENCHIEMSEE, SAAL MIT DEM OCHSENAUGE.

Around us in this long *Marmorhalle* were walls and pillars of what seemed costly marble, but proved to be only a good imitation thereof. On the ceiling above us were frescos of Europe, Asia, Africa, and America in allegorical figures, and around us were colossal statues. Our guide led us on through the *Hartschier Saal*, hung with gold-embroidered blue velvet, where he pointed out a cabinet of tortoise-shell, valued at a sum which we translated into nineteen thousand dollars. From thence we passed through the *Grosser Vorsaal*, or waiting-room, which is lined with Scajola marble, and hung with lilac damask, gold-embroidered, into the *Saal mit dem Ochsenauge*, the handsome salon, and a vivid reminder of Versailles. Around us were pictures portraying scenes in the life of Louis Quatorze; and at one end was a small bronze equestrian statue of that gay monarch. Over the green and gold damask, and lace hangings, our party fell into ecstasies of admiration, as they did over the beautiful *plafond* above our heads, painted by Edward Schwoiser, whereon, in melting, glowing forms, Aurora takes in marriage the Star-god, Astrios.

Wondering at the French character of our surroundings, we were glad to be told by the guide that although the architects visited Versailles when making the plans for the palace, yet architects, designers, painters, cabinet-makers, and workmen were all from Munich. Of the three hundred embroideresses who worked here for seven years, one afterward became our teacher in Hanover.

With a fresh accession of dignity our guide ushered us into the sanctuary of the *Punktzimmer*, — or best bedroom, where mortal never dared to sleep, — and there we stood mute, in front of the gilded railing which enclosed the great gilded bed surmounted by a huge, gilded crown, upheld by Cupids and finished by clusters of white ostrich plumes. At one side of the bed was a gilded dressing-table laden with rich, gilded toilet articles and a gilded *prie-dieu* and *fauteuils*. Great gilded candelabra stood on either side of the bed, and a large crystal chandelier hung in the centre of the room, and the curtains here were of red velvet.

With true American instinct, we computed the cost of this room to be eight hundred and twenty thousand dollars. Stumbling on over the slippery floors through Louis's smaller and more habitable private apartments, we were shown the bed in which he really slept thirty-six times, his marble bath, and the dining-table, which, all set for dinner, came up through the floor by machinery.

Breathless from the excitement of so much magnificence, we strolled slowly back to the *restauration*, and sat there awhile, sipping our coffee and crumbling our little sweet cakes, and looked back at the palace, which stood deserted and embosomed in foliage, like Dornröschen's castle of fairy tale.

Talking of Louis II. and Elizabeth, the little maid whom he loved and who died (according to a veracious paper booklet purchased at the station), we took little note of time, and were obliged to make a hurried start to catch our train. Indeed, so great was our haste and so sudden our awakening from dreams of romance, that we took the wrong train and steamed away for hours in the opposite direction, nearly reaching Salzburg before we discovered our mistake. We did not much regret the blunder, for we were rewarded by a lovely view of the Tyrolese Alps in the sunset light, and a glimpse of peasant life at the little inn at Rosenheim, where we stopped a few minutes.

At eleven o'clock that night we re-entered the *pension* in Munich to be greeted by our landlady, who seemed glad that something at the last had gone wrong, according to her predictions.

ISARTHOR, MUNICH.

MUNICH AND FRANKFORT.

WE had been refreshed by a drive in the Englischer Garten in Munich and along the Gasteig promenade; and now, feeling the need of mental nourishment, we turned our steps in the direction of the library for an hour or so's browsing among old books and illuminations. We had heard "Lohengrin" badly sung the evening before, and had pronounced the opera-house ugly, bare, and dirty; but now, as we ascended the wide flight of steps, we exclaimed in admiration at the dignified, noble pillars around us and at the vaulting of the ceiling. Two stately statues pointed to the open door, and through it we passed into the large, light, airy room filled with treasures in the shape of illuminated missals and early printed books. The glory of color in the painted parchments attracted us to the glass cases at the farther end of the room, and there we lingered, studying out the delicate scrollwork and beautiful little birds and animals, and the monogram A. D. at the foot of the page of one, which tells that Albrecht Dürer delighted in illuminating a prayer-book for the Emperor Maximilian I., sometime in the year 1550. Ah, if we could only have turned the page, and have seen a little more! I suppose the custodian does unlock the case once a year and turn over a page, so that the good people of Munich may by degrees and in yearly instalments see all the book.

Egeria and I, however, could not stay in Munich indefinitely for years; and we turned with a sigh to the guide, who had been napping in an armchair, and, evidently wakened by our voices, came forward and persisted in turning our attention to the case of Florentine illuminations, done fifty years later than Dürer's, and though graceful and flowery, yet lacking the vigor and clearness of his outlines. And, yes, we were glad to see the first Gutenberg Bible, printed in 1450, and the rude old written breviary of Alaric, King of the Visigoths in the sixth century, and also the first Latin Bible printed in

Munich, and another illuminated prayer-book made in Nuremberg.

In a case at our left were mementos of another great German, — Martin Luther, — his letters, manuscripts, and his big Bible, with fine portraits by Kranach of Luther and his disciple, Melancthon. A young attendant was showing three enthusiastic old English ladies through the library, and, I fear, had been imposing some wonderful stories on their simplicity; for he was so amused at their comments that he smiled at us as we passed them. Dear rosy-cheeked old dames! I wonder whether, on going back to England, they took up the study of German history!

There are in the Munich Library valuable theological collections; but theology was too hearty a meal for our mental appetite that day, and leaving behind the heavy volumes with a shudder, we passed into the street.

Some people told us it was folly to go to Frankfort-on-the-Maine; but having two or three unoccupied days on our plan, we wrote in the word "Frankfort," and there we were, as much bound to spend those days in Frankfort as if we belonged to a veritable party of " Cookies."

Well, I suppose we were foolish in our choice of a hotel, for, although comfortable in every way, yet on our first appearance in the dining-room in the Hotel de l'Union, we found only one other lady at the table. Some sort of business or manufacturers' convention was in progress in Frankfort, and down the two long tables were rows of jolly, red, masculine German faces. One had an opportunity to study every variety of beard and moustache, the swishing of German soup-swallowing, and what was to me a peculiarly interesting mode of eating asparagus, — throwing the head back, poising the right hand holding the asparagus lightly in the air, the little finger well in evidence, and then slowly absorbing every atom of the delicate stalk. Some of the older men had grown very proficient in this exercise. The manufacturers were so engrossed by their business, their jokes, and, finally, their cigars, that they were oblivious of us, and the head waiter was so attentive that we decided to stay. "Would the gracious ladies care to visit the electrical exhibition that evening?" No, the gracious ladies were tired; but what amusement was there for to-morrow? No concerts; ah, a pantomime of "Aschenbrödel" in the fine new opera-house. The morning was devoted to Dannecker's beautiful Ariadne; and the afternoon found us seated in the opera-house, surrounded by a large Hebrew concourse, and nearly as much interested in the children in the audience as in those on the stage. Cinderella was a dainty, refined little person; and her Prince, in white attire, "sighing like a furnace," in imitation of Shakespeare's lover, was all that could be desired. The prettiest scene was the dance of the Heinzelmännchen, who came to do Cinderella's work in the kitchen, while she tripped off to the ball. Eighty children in all were on the stage, and all danced. The Brownies, building the fire and stirring the great caldron, danced; the one inside the lamp danced; the plates on the dresser danced; and the Brownies riding up and down on machinery in the big churn, kept time to the music, while the children in the audience were uproarious in their applause. Another pretty bit was when the godmother transformed the rat in the trap to a chubby, little sweet-faced *Kutscher* about seven years old, in scarlet livery, and the lizard into a little footman in green, and with great complacency the two took their places on the fairy coach. When Cinderella escaped from the ball at midnight, she ran over a long bridge, followed by the Prince and by Siphax, the little German Puck. This tricksy sprite touched with his wand the bridge, which broke in the middle, letting down the stepmother and the wicked sisters, the King and all his court ladies and gentlemen, who were pursuing in hot haste. The last gentleman went down head first and heels in the air, and in their satins and velvets, all floundered about in the ditch below.

After the final apotheosis of Aschenbrödel amid fairies, flowers, and electric lights, we two escaped into a blinding snow-storm, cabless and tramless, to walk some blocks to our hotel, incurring what proved to be our only European experience of colds and sore throats.

The following day we drove over the

stone bridge to the suburb of Sachsenhausen, and saw there two of the nine gates that form the entrance to the town. Not equal, we decided, to the *Isarthor*, that we had admired so much in Munich. The Maine is interesting from its historic associations, and so is the *Römer*, or council-house, where the German emperors were formerly elected. In the imperial hall are paintings on the wall of full-length portraits of the emperors,— from Conrad I. to Francis II. In the election-chapel of the cathedral of St. Bartholomew, the emperor was formerly elected, and afterward crowned in front of the high altar. Literary and commercial, but not military, are the inhabitants of Frankfort, and we saw none of the distinguished officers that we had constantly met in the streets in Munich. Quite important are they, for the army of Bavaria has a special place in the army of

GERMAN BEER-GARDEN.

United Germany, and is under the jurisdiction of the King of Bavaria.

Johann Wolfgang von Goethe was born in Frankfort; and to and through his father's house we went, being specially interested in the souvenirs of Lili, his vivacious Frankfort friend. "Goethe had many loves," remarked the guide, apologetically, as he pointed out the various articles in the case, — verses, miniatures, and snuff-boxes. There were many records of the twenty years the poet spent in Frankfort, the earliest being a set of little garments worn at a very early age. The old German kitchen of his mother, Elizabeth Textor, showed that she looked well to the ways of her household, being as capable in putting up sweetmeats as she was in instilling noble thoughts into the mind of her son.

AUTUMN DAYS IN NUREMBERG AND WEIMAR.

IN the autumn, on our way north to Hanover, we stopped for a few days in Nuremberg, and found pleasant quarters in the Bayerischer Hof, which is said to be five hundred years old. Under our windows were little covered bridges across the river, and in the market-place near were picturesque booths. The air, both on the bridge leading to the town and in the market-place, was anything but salubrious; and we concluded that life in an unsanitary mediæval town might have its disadvantages. Who could say what fevers and malaria lurked in the walls of those quaint, gabled houses, where wrought iron arms held curious lamps, and statues

NASSAU HOUSE, NUREMBERG.

of saints and graceful figures of the Virgin adorned the corner buildings! The castle with its torture-chamber formed our first attraction. The castle of Nuremberg has been introduced by Dürer into more than one of his engravings; and Holbein the younger also painted it as background in one of the two panels which flank his Saint Sebastian, the one in which Saint Elizabeth tends a blind beggar with the face of Holbein himself. In the Hangman's Tower were displayed the instruments of torture by means of which the "painful question" was put to the accused. Before the actual applying of physical torture came the mental torturing by the sharp judge, when fear sometimes effected the same results as the rack and thumb-screw. The iron Virgin, a figure which opened to receive its victim, whose eyes and breast were then penetrated by iron spikes, was the most repellent and therefore the most interesting thing in the collection. A cradle studded with iron spikes also held our attention for some time; and we wondered at the age that used such means of punishment, and that burned Jerome and Huss for preaching against the law of torture. A pretty, smiling young German girl showed us through the gloomy rooms and seemed to accentuate the horror of her surroundings.

A far more agreeable place we found the Germanisches Museum, an old stone monastic building with mullioned windows, used to hold the pictures and statues of mediæval German artists. Among the pictures, I remember chiefly the Madonna with the Pea-blossom, by Meister Wilhelm of Cologne, and among the statues, the Virgin carved in wood by Veit Stoss, which stands in the chapel. Along the cloisters were stone figures of old Saxon kings and queens; one of a Queen

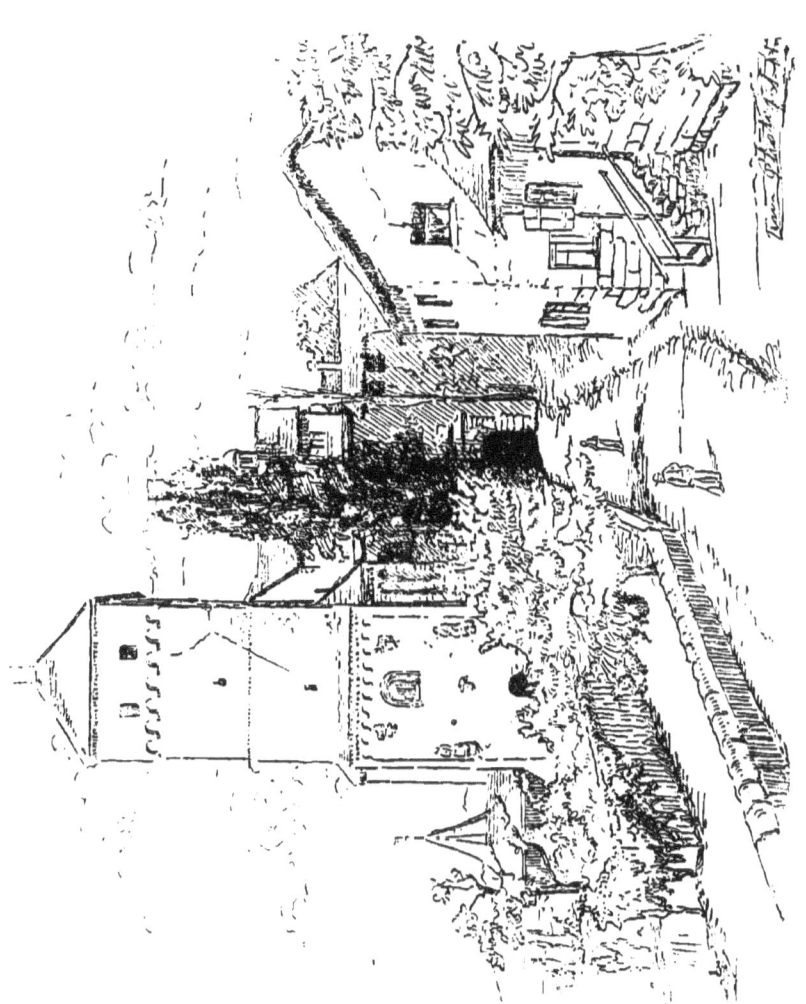

KAISERBURG, NEAR NUREMBERG.

Matilda had a really lovely face. Stained glass windows opened on the court; and crests and coats-of-arms of the Hohenzollern family were prominent among the designs on the colored panes.

An artist was standing in the court copying these armorial bearings, as we crossed and entered the room filled with relics of the Swiss Lake-dwellers and little models of prehistoric houses made of logs intersected with stones and roofed with straw. Logs from an old Roman bridge at Mayence brought us somewhat farther down into actual history; and in the adjoining room we found copies of the gold vessels of King Athanarich, and the silver treasure-chest of the Holy Roman Empire. Here were barbaric gold and gems of the days of Charlemagne and Barbarossa, camp-altars and church services, reminders of Masses before battle and thanksgiving hymns after victory.

Scarcely milder in tone or in suggested story were the relics of one who wielded a mightier weapon than the sword, — the manuscript letters of Martin Luther.

The name of all others connected with Nuremberg is of course that of Albrecht Dürer ; and we duly visited his house with its old German interior, and longed to carry away the grotesque wooden candelabrum in shape of a three-headed dragon in the hall. From there our pilgrimage led us to the Bratwürstglöcklein, the little tavern next the chapel of St. Moritz, where Dürer used to meet the handsome, white-bearded Peter Vischer, the poet Hans Sachs, and the sculptor Adam Krafft. While the sausages were roasting at the fire, and the foaming beer was being poured into the tall mugs, the group of artists discussed the pictures, the carvings, the statues, and the songs which they were making, as well as the municipal affairs of the city, whose prosperity was largely due to their calm judgment and clear-sighted wisdom. The smiling aspect of the trim little cemetery made it seem as if the word "emigravit" on the tombstone was correct, — as if Nuremberg were waiting for the Dürer who departed to return and develop and perfect his art and his city.

Weimar, of which Goethe said, " I have lived here fifty years, and where have I not been? but I was always glad to return to Weimar." The magic of the name and the desire to see the Goethe memorials induced us to stop in the little German town; but we could not stay long enough to explore the environs and learn the charm which a residence of fifty years made more intense. The theatre was closed, so we were not able to see any representation of the drama while there.

In the little shop near the hotel were copies of the glorious bust of Goethe as

Apollo, made during his travels in Italy as a young man, and endless photographs of the pictures of Hermann and Dorothea and Faust and Margaret. The noble statue of the two friends, Goethe and Schiller, was sufficiently life-like, though larger than life in size, to bring the two men before us, as they trod the shaded streets in the days of their youth and genius. And the town house of Goethe was filled with mementos of the poet and associations of his life there. The Ducal Museum, too, contained much that was interesting in porcelain and statues; Thorwalden's Ganymede finding special favor in our eyes. But the chief interest and beauty of Weimar is the park. It was arranged and laid out by Goethe; and here he and Schiller bathed in the Ilm in the time when cold-water bathing was rarely practised in Germany. The beeches, the pines, the elms, the chestnuts, the trees of

GOETHE AND SCHILLER STATUE, WEIMAR.

mountain-ash, with their brilliant berries that fill the park, are lovely in their own loveliness; but the crowning glory of the park is found in the spreading branches of the linden-trees. A softness in the drooping of the boughs, a certain elegance of outline, a pervading air of old-world sentiment, made us feel that these were indeed the trees under whose shade sat and strolled Goethe and Frau von Stein and Karl August and the noble Duchess Luise. Near the Ilm stood the little bark house where the Duke often lived, and in sight of this was the Garden House where Goethe lived for seven years. The garden where he wrote, and studied plant life, the orchard, and the arrangement of the house — all show the simplicity of the poet's tastes. A stone bench in the garden was inscribed with a verse containing a play on the name Von Stein; and as his letters to this lady contain so many details of eating and drinking, we may be sure that the table near the bench often held a substantial lunch. We were destined later to meet, not a descendant of the charming and witty Frau von Stein, nor a distant relative of the lovely Duchess of Saxe-Weimar, whom Napoleon respected as a noble adversary, but a lady who lived in Weimar, and who, by this title, as well as by her own sweet manners, recalled to us the eighteenth-century names, and events connected with the home of Goethe.

HANOVER.

HANOVER is especially desirable as a place of residence for foreigners, on account of the purity of the German spoken there. The advantages offered to musical students are many and varied. The opera supported by the government is remarkably good, and both singers and members of the orchestra are able to supplement their salaries by fees received from music lessons.

We were settled in a German family, where were living several English girls who were seriously studying music, devoting six or eight hours a day to the piano, the violin, the 'cello, and the cultivation of the voice. German was the language of the family, and she who would not speak

German must perforce remain silent. Therefore we spoke German.

And German it is necessary to speak in the streets, the shops, and the theatre; for although the English clergyman has been a resident of Hanover for forty years, the English colony is comparatively small, and except ourselves there were but two Americans in the city. During the winter we were there, an unusually large number of Americans were studying at Göttingen, where the women of Germany are forbidden to present themselves as students, although American women are always welcomed.

In Hanover, the police regulations are enforced as strictly as they are in other German cities. All foreigners are required to live agreeably to the *Polizei*, closing their pianos at ten o'clock in the evening, keeping mindful watch of their stove-fires, and having always ready for inspection the papers stating the age, sex, profession, personal appearance, and future prospects in life of the stranger within the gates. So we felt that all our actions were known to the authorities, and that, as we had been told in Venice, if friends wished to find us, it was only necessary to inquire at the police station to learn all particulars as to our whereabouts.

Beside the police, Hanover is strictly guarded by the officers and soldiers of the garrison; and it is rather a favorite joke of the Emperor to appear suddenly and unannounced in their midst, hoping to surprise the members of his army in some neglect of their duty. But to the honor of the commanding officer be it said, that so far from being found derelict, every such occasion has shown his subalterns to be on guard and prepared for assault. Waterloo Place, the square on which stands the picturesque castle, is now used as a parade-ground, and here is the Waterloo column, surmounted by a figure of Victory, and inscribed with the names of the Hanoverians who fell in the battle.

Shortly after our arrival, the Emperor came to Hanover for the military manœuvres, and the hunting steaks from the wild boar shot by the imperial hunter were served at our table; and though we had no opportunity of watching the manœuvres, yet we went one evening to the opera purposely to see the Emperor, and were fortunate in securing places near the imperial *loge*. So delighted was Egeria with the conduct and personal appearance of Wilhelm II., that, in similar circumstances, I think she would have acted as did an American lady in Dresden, who loudly professed democratic principles, but after having been graciously recognized by the Emperor at a ball, was observed to express herself very differently in regard to principalities and powers. There was a group of officers in the Emperor's *loge;* and hearty laughter and applause showed that the efforts of the singers were appreciated. The opera commanded for that evening was "Cavalleria Rusticana," or "Sicilian Peasant-honor," as it was called in Germany; and the musical farce preceding it dealt with the doings of a Cadi who was made ridiculous by the plottings of the other characters. The proceeds went to the pension-fund of the theatre. Hans von Bülow was once director of the Hanoverian opera, and it has enjoyed special prestige, as the King of Hanover was particularly fond of music, and spent nearly every evening at the opera.

We also went frequently to the Symphony Concerts given by the Capelle, or band of a fusileer regiment on Wednesday afternoons. We enjoyed the freedom of the large open room of the concert-house, where people sat in groups, the men smoking, and the women busy with embroidery, and where you are at liberty to come in late, and also to leave early, if you choose. The latter is a desirable privilege, for the tobacco-smoke becomes almost unendurable toward the end of the programme.

In the old part of the town are several interesting Gothic houses dating from the olden time, and the red brick market church is a quaint building, near which stands the statue of a former pastor noted for his benevolence. The castle church is only interesting from the fact that the Electress Sophia and her son George I. are buried in its vaults. There are picturesque bits in places along the banks of the Leine; and on a winter afternoon there is no gayer, brighter street than the

OLD CHURCH AND GOTHIC HOUSES, HANOVER.

Georg Strasse, the shop-windows attractively decorated, and the frequenters of the Café Robby finding amusement in watching the throng of passers-by.

Opposite us, on the Mitburgerdamm, was a large *Diakonissenanstalt;* and we watched with interest what could be learned from the windows of the life of the hospital. The deaconesses looked strong, capable women with happy, interested faces. They say they are too busy to launder and crimp white starched caps, or arrange the folds of long veils, so the hair is neatly arranged in bands, on either side of the face, and surmounted by an ugly, stiff black bonnet. When Christmas drew near, the deaconesses were busily employed in making decorations for the Christmas-tree, — white paper lilies and roses with centres of gold thread, — and while they worked, they sang their Christmas carols. There were little garments made, also, for the waxen figure of the Child in the Manger. Among the many good works carried on by the deaconesses, there is, at Bielefeld on the Rhine, a village of eight thousand epileptic persons, where workshops, schools, concert-halls, and churches are all successfully carried on; and the community, notwithstanding the painful character of the disease from which its members suffer, is a happy and prosperous one.

Two interesting pictures in the Museum at Hanover attracted us. One portrays an event in the Seven Years' War, in which a Hanoverian lady takes part; and the other is Ittenbach's picture of the youthful Virgin. The fair-haired little figure stands looking upward with clasped hands, youth and innocence in every line of the face. The rose-colored scarf, that encircles the head instead of the customary virginal veil, floats back against the gold flower-stamped background, where the halo bears the words, "Sancta Maria Virgo." The picture has much of the feeling of the work of the old Italian masters. There may also be seen in the Museum curious old German costumes, silver jewelry, and armor, and carved furniture of antique design.

Through the long double avenue of lime-trees, we drove out two miles to visit the royal palace of Herrenhausen, dear to lovers of English history and the Protestant succession. Built by George I. whose father Ernest, the great Elector, promulgated a decree in 1688, threatening the gallows to duellists, because, as he expresses it, "revenge is reserved to God alone, and we thus incite God's just anger on our land and people, by placing our own souls, so dearly bought by Christ, in apparent danger." The palace was also a favorite residence of George II. It is a long, low building, and we found little to admire in the architecture. The orchid-houses are kept up, but the flowers of course are reserved. There were historical portraits in the picture-gallery, some by Sir Peter Lely, the German artist who, transferring his talents to the English court, painted for Charles I., Cromwell, and Charles II. We were later to become very familiar with a picture of his in England, — a graceful figure of Nell Gwynne, to which we became so attached that hereafter we shall always think kindly of the subject as well as of the picture. The gardens were really pretty. The straight walks were lined with clipped, formal hedges, and had flower-beds, where a few late flowers were still blooming, and in one place was a turf-carpeted sylvan theatre, where the ladies and gentlemen of the court used to act in Schiller's plays. At the end of a gravelled walk is a seated

CHARACTER HEAD, HANOVER.

statue of the Electress Sophia, who died
suddenly, while sitting in these gardens,
and in the Mausoleum is a fine recumbent figure of Queen Frederica, by Rauch.
The trees of course were bare, but we
could understand that in summer the leafy
avenues had a beauty of their own.

Hildesheim, they told us, was a curious
old town, and called the birthplace of
German art. The excursion could be made
in an afternoon; so thither we went to see
the ancient cathedral and the rose-tree
eight hundred years old. In the square,
the street of the old market, and the street
back of it, are curious houses, showing
obsolete styles of domestic architecture;
and in the Langenhagen is the residence
of some notability who was honored by an
entire façade of carved stone-work. The
old German character is sustained throughout the town, even the new buildings
being built in imitation of the old, and

the hotel, where we stopped for an hour's rest, being furnished throughout with *altdeutsch* stoves, chimney-pieces, and wood-work.

The cathedral seemed to us older than anything we had yet seen in Germany; in fact, it dates from the eleventh century. Bishop Bernward, the ruler of this episcopal city of fifteen thousand inhabitants, was himself a worker in gold filigree for the ornamentation of chalices and crucifixes; and the art which he encouraged prospered in Hildesheim, and rich examples of it are still to be seen in the Treasury. The brazen column of Bishop Bernward, in the cathedral place, bears in bas-relief many small figures illustrating the events of Our Lord's Life and Passion. Within the cathedral itself and in the more perfect Romanesque church of St. Godehard are richly carved capitals, alabaster pillars dating from pagan Saxon times, massive brazen fonts, and curious enamels. The cloister impressed us with a sense of its antiquity; and when we descended into the crypt to touch the branches of the rose-tree that still grows against the wall, from the choir above our heads burst out the sonorous voices of the priests chanting the vesper service. With the name of Hildesheim will ever be associated a never-to-be-forgotten picture of gray antiquity.

The short December days grew shorter and shorter, and the climate, never good, grew worse, and the zephyrs, never balmy, turned to rough winds, and we knew that Christmas was approaching. We knew it, too, by the appearance of the confectioners' windows. Mammoth cakes, pronounced *grossartig* by admiring children, appeared, flanked by grotesque figures of animals, fruits, and vegetables made of *marzipan*, — a composition of almond meal and rose-water, so called because it was formerly made on St. Mark's Day. And the fact was also apparent from the forest of Christmas trees that suddenly seemed to grow in the streets.

On the eve of the festival, we ventured on an excursion through the crowded streets, stopping in the market to see the booths where toys and decorations for the *Weihnachtsbaüme* were sold, and peeping into the lighted windows of houses where blazed, in greater or less splendor, the Christmas tree. At the Lutheran church near us, a service was in progress, and we made our way through the throng in the churchyard (where Goethe's Lotte is buried) into the building, to hear the children tell the Christmas story and sing the sweet German carols. Then we went home to our own tree and gifts and story-telling. Tales of the Harz, the spectral mists that surround the Brocken, and legends of the mountains of south Germany enlivened our evening. The gayest was that of the Countess Kunigunde, who, although young and beautiful, desired to remain unmarried, and therefore declared that she would wed only the lover who should ride round the castle on the top of the outer wall. As might be expected, most of her suitors retired on this announcement. A few, however, made the attempt, and were dashed to pieces in the abyss. Finally a knight presented himself whose manners and appearance touched the heart of Kunigunde, and she joyfully watched him make the dangerous ride in safety. Yet when she advanced to greet her bridegroom, instead of a kiss, she received a smart box on the ear, and his parting words told the inconsolable Kunigunde that he was Albert of Thuringia, who, leaving at home a beauteous wife, had come thus to avenge the cruel death of a younger brother.

Such was and such is the German estimate of the lady who, turning from all thoughts of *Verlobung und Heirath*, prefers to braid her hair in tresses dedicated to Saint Catherine, or cut it off altogether, in the fashion that indicates serious devotion to a profession and an independent, solitary life.

A GERMAN CAFÉ.

IDLE MOMENTS IN GERMAN CAFÉS.

"IT is the fair acceptance makes the perfect entertainment, not the cates." And so, with fair acceptance, did we enjoy many moments spent in German cafés. Indeed, the cates are a minor part of café life, for one may sit for an hour over a cup of coffee, an ice, or even a glass of soda-water. There are the comic and the daily papers to be looked over, the decorations of the café,—sometimes Old German, sometimes Renaissance—to be admired and criticised, and the animated crowd of "all sorts and conditions of men" and women to be studied. The smallest, yet perhaps the most homelike, was the little Café Robby in Hanover. How pleasant it was to sit there in the winter afternoon with our embroidery, and watch through the wide glass windows of the octagonal little building the élite of Hanover, — officers, ladies, professors, opera-singers, — passing along the Georg Strasse. There we used to read the English papers, which we saw nowhere else; and often, just before going to the opera, we stopped at the bright, cheery, business-like little place for coffee and *Kuchen*. I fear our transatlantic memories are forever connected with eating, for our first question, on arriving in a new place, was for the name of the best *Conditor*, *Patissier*, or Pastry-cook, all in capital letters, such importance did they assume in our minds.

Happy, too, are the souvenirs of the German Crêmerie in Geneva. After a long walk of some miles along the shore of the lake, or an excursion to Coppet or Ferney, what more acceptable than a cup of chocolate, a glass of milk, or a bottle of

A GERMAN WAITRESS.

Swiss wine at the Crêmerie? Of papers, only the "Fliegende Blätter" was to be found there, and on the little side street there was no view from the windows; but proper Genevese ladies came there, and young girls studying in Geneva, and elderly English gentlemen, and sometimes a couple of German officers temporarily in Geneva for the purpose of learning French. It was very quiet, restful, and orderly in the Crêmerie, and there we could sit and discuss the last opera or the latest sensation, or practise conversational German by chatting with the young girls in attendance.

Having an hour or two in Leipsic, we spent some of our time in a café, and being midday, we ordered *bifteck*, *salat*, and beer. We had accepted our cab-driver's recommendation to the best *restauration* in Leipsic, yet as opinions differ on cafés as on other matters, it was with dubious satisfaction that we entered the garden and selected a little table neatly decked in white. But we did not linger over our luncheon, for the waiter was somewhat impertinent, and a noisy party of Germans were quarrelling at the table next us — was it over the printing and publishing of Leipsic books? At the time of the Easter Fair, the booksellers of Germany assemble here to settle their annual accounts, for the whole book trade of the country is centred in this spot, and even the booksellers of adjoining countries have agents here. In the hot, dusty rooms inside the café, more publishers and booksellers were discussing national affairs in high-pitched voices. But perhaps it was a party of musicians, and not booksellers, who were assembled that day in the café.

Had we been men, we certainly would have visited the beer-cellars, for a beer-cellar, and not a café, has the artist given

GERMAN BEER-CELLAR.

us in our illustration. The most celebrated German beer-cellar is in Leipsic, — Auerbach's cellar, — a vault under an old house in the market-place. In this room is laid the scene of one act of Faust, in which the students are supplied by Mephistopheles with various kinds of wine, drawn from holes bored with a gimlet in the table. It is said that when studying at Leipsic University, Goethe often tested the quality of the wine at this famous cellar.

When we reached Munich, we were told that the most sumptuous of German cafés was directly under our *pension* on the Brienner Strasse. Accordingly, one evening we all descended to the Café Luitpold, chaperoned by our landlady. An air of smartness, elegance, and even coquetry pervaded the place; and the composition mouldings of Renaissance figures, flowers, and foliage on walls, ceiling, and chimney-piece, were rich and florid. Mirrors and furniture were all of Renaissance design; and we wished that the pretty Fräulein who served us could have been put in corresponding costume. A glimpse into the billiard-room showed more elaborate decoration and more comfortable lounging-places.

People in evening dress arrived from the theatres, causing greater bustle and activity among the corps of attendants. Two ladies seated themselves at a table near us and ordered such an elaborate repast, including so many and various wines, that we watched their progress with interest, as we dallied over our ices. Although not in mediæval costume, still the attendants, both men and women, were smartly dressed, and moved gracefully about under the electric lights, or leaned against the columns in studied poses during the intervals of serving. Still, notwithstanding all the gorgeousness of dress and decoration, the *pour-boire* was not forgotten, as we found on leaving that more than one Fraulein stood in our way with open palm.

ON THE LAKE OF GENEVA.

SWISS SAIL-BOAT.

WE went from Paris to Geneva in the autumn, and found ourselves pleasantly settled on the Rue du Montblanc. From our windows we looked up the street to the railway station, and down the street to the Jardin Anglais and the Pont Mont Blanc. There were Russians, Greeks, Germans, French, and English in the house, but we lived rather quietly in our own little salon, where some friends came constantly to enjoy our fire of *briquettes* and our flowers, or we visited them in their salon at the other end of the hall, where there was the attraction of a piano. Long walks into the country around filled our afternoons, — strolls along the Savoy side of the lake, wanderings on the Swiss side, past the many châteaux and villas, where we speculated as to the inhabitants and their manner of life, and criticised those who passed us in carriages or on horseback. We loitered in the grounds of the Ariana Museum, where we picked sprigs of holly, and came home in the late dusk along the trim Geneva streets, feeling safe and free among the Switzers, and walked along the lamp-lighted quays as fearlessly as we did at noonday. Honest, kindly folk, the Genevese. What wonder that men of letters, political refugees and exiles from all lands, love to linger among them for a while, enjoying Swiss honey and Swiss bread, cleanliness, comfort, and repose! There had been an anarchist red-flag procession, they told us, on the first day of the preceding May, but it had been quite as peaceful as that of the Fête des Vignerons, and we had some difficulty in learning the name of the President of the Swiss Confederation. Helvetic politics are evidently quite different from those of other lands. A recently elected member of the Council was escorted with banners and music through the streets one day; but the election had been calm and peaceful, and there were no campaign speeches, no scandals as to the private life of the candidates, apparently no bribery and corruption, — in short, no fun to a lover of election-time in the land of the stars and stripes. There is a simple, honest, and childlike quality about the Swiss, which at the first glimpse hardly accords with their well-known sturdiness and vigor of mind. Zurich is renowned as a seat of learning, and the lecture-rooms of the University of Geneva are crowded with students. Their graduates have become famous for scientific achievements, and among their number are many distinguished engineers and able physicians. As theologians, musicians, and leaders in education, they have made their mark; and the little land may well be proud of her sons.

Its red-crossed flag floats proudly in the breeze, and under its protection we felt a degree of security not known elsewhere in Europe. Our favorite walk was along the shores of the blue lake, or over the Pont Mont Blanc, where we often lingered to feed the tame swans and gulls gathered on the water below. The Rhone divides Geneva into two parts. On the left bank is the old town with narrow streets, its old clock-tower, and on the hill the Hotel de Ville and the cathedral of St. Pierre. In the open market-place were booths with objects of all sorts exposed for sale, and on Saturdays there was a gorgeous display of chrysanthemums. The country people came in to buy from these stalls; but the Genevese preferred to buy what they needed at the handsome shops on the Quai des Bergues, where jewelry, watches, bric-à-brac, Swiss carvings, musical boxes, and meerschaum pipes are attractively displayed. The fur-shop of Geneva is quite celebrated, and we heard of ladies who preferred Genevese dressmakers to those of Paris.

The opera-house is modelled after that of Paris; and so fond are the Genevese of their theatrical entertainments that the building is ventilated and the temperature regulated by law. There are two classes in Genevese society, — those who keep

Sunday according to the old Calvinistic ideas, and those who, more liberally inclined, as were our hostesses, attend a long morning service at the cathedral, spend the afternoon at the opera, and in the evening entertain their acquaintances with games and dancing and cards.

Of course we found our way to the cathedral, and sat in Calvin's chair, and saw the pulpit where he used to preach. We wondered if the sermon usually lasted four hours, as did that of a certain English Archbishop, who merely remarked at the conclusion that he was a little tired from standing so long. Severe indeed must have been the rule of the two austere Frenchmen, Farel and Calvin; stiff and unbending their doctrines as the Genevan bands their theology introduced. Although banished for a few years, yet on his return to Geneva, Calvin's power became paramount and lasted for many years after his death.

Within two centuries a great change came over the spirit of the Genevese; and without injustice to Calvin's nobler aims, a wise tolerance succeeded to the relentless severity of the earlier time. It seems like retributive justice, or the irony of fate, that for over a century this stronghold of intolerance and unyielding dogmatism should have become the refuge for theological and political dissent of every degree. Into this peaceful eddy, political refugees have drifted from every corner of Europe, and the air of Calvin's city is filled with memories of Rousseau, Voltaire, and Gibbon. Over a little chain bridge is Rousseau's Isle, and on it is the well-known seated bronze statue of the author of "Emile." Not far away is Voltaire's retreat at Ferney; and at Lausanne, Gibbon wrote the greater part of his monumental history.

We were taken by a poet-friend to see

ROUSSEAU'S ISLE.

the meeting of the waters of the Rhone and the Aar, and to hear quotations from Moore's verses on the meeting of the waters in the Vale of Avoca, — for our friend had travelled in Ireland, — and to lament over the unpicturesque aspect of the road we had to traverse. And many times did we linger before the windows of the handsome shops on the Grand Quai, and often did we visit one special and tempting little shop for the sale of antiquities, on the Quai des Bergues. Here one of the party bought, regretting it afterward, two great dusty volumes of an old French edition of " Don Quixote," and another purchased old silver *bijouterie;* and I found a little tea-cup, treasured still, that was made near by, at Nyon, when the royal porcelain factory at Sèvres was closed during the Revolution, and the artists fled to Switzerland, there to continue their work.

Equally, of course, we took the excursion up the lake to Chillon, counting the lateen sails, as we passed them, and looking back at the panorama of the mountain group,— Mont Blanc, the Aiguilles Rouge, the Aiguille du Midi, the long line of the Voirons, and the lower slope of the Grand and Petit Salève, to whose summit we hoped to climb. I fear that we did not feel in the least poetical or romantic at Chillon, nor did the solitary English lady who joined us, and who was chiefly concerned as to the exact amount the boatman had cheated us, as we guessed from the glances that passed between him and the *gens d'armes*. Nor romantically impressed seemed the St. Bernard puppy with whom I stayed while the others visited the dungeons and enjoyed thrills at bygone cruelties, while the St. Bernard and I enjoyed the fresh air, the sunshine, and the glorious wild mountain-land at that end of the lake.

Then, too, I must not forget one sober Sunday afternoon spent at Coppet, where we wandered through the old-fashioned gardens where Madame de Staël once entertained Madame Récamier, De Chateaubriand, and Byron. Before that time, her father, M. Necker, a native of Geneva, and his lovely wife, whom Gibbon had once released from a marriage-engagement, when he "sighed as a lover, but obeyed as a son," had lived here. The château was undergoing a grand cleaning in preparation for the coming of Madame d'Haussonville, the present proprietor; so we peeped inside at the bust of Necker and stared at the chickens in the old courtyard, where vines grew over the trellis, and flowers bloomed in the beds. The exterior of the château was severely plain, a coat-of-arms over the doorway, and in the corners, water-pipes ran down from the eaves. Outside the iron gates we met an old man, who told us, whether truthfully or not I cannot say, that he remembered having once seen Madame Récamier. As we strolled along the broad walks of the park, a friendly Newfoundland joined us and volunteered his services as guide. So rambling along the borders of a brook, and over rustic bridges, and stopping to rest on carved stone seats, we played out a little comedy. I was the hostess, Madame de Staël; the poet was M. de Chateaubriand; a dark-eyed little lady was Madame Récamier; and a gay young Austrian was an attaché paying an afternoon call at the château. Poetry, of course, was our theme, and Napoleon and Talleyrand were not once mentioned.

THE ESCALADE.

ON the 6th of December, 1610, the Genevans successfully resisted the attack of the Savoyards, who attempted to scale the fortifications of the town; and the women of Geneva, young and old, appeared on the ramparts and poured kettlefuls of boiling water and melted lead on the heads of the invaders. Wherefore to-day in Geneva, when the time draws near to the 6th of December, you may see in all the shop-windows little and big chocolate kettles known as "marmites," and you may hear sung on the streets snatches of the Song of the Escalade. For this bulwark of the Reformed Church, which was fortified so strongly by the Protestant princes, to

were assured that with a strong escort the thing might be done; and every able-bodied bachelor at the table at once volunteered his services to form part of our guard. Of course the married people were already provided for, and with a strong *esprit de corps* they kept together, while our party numbered five "unprotected females," three of whom were very young and more than very pretty, and were considered to be under our chaperonage.

The 6th of December arrived, heralded, as I have said, by the notes of Escalade songs and the appearance of the candy kettles in the confectioners' windows. We spent the day as usual, and met at supper-time in the *salle à manger*, where tables, both long and small, presented a festal appearance. I had begged for a quiet little table apart, and that evening we found our party

increased by the addition of an English
gentleman who had been crowded out
from the long table. He, however, seemed
no whit abashed by his feminine surroundings; but entering into the spirit of the
occasion, we discussed our good things,
clinked our champagne glasses, toasting
the memory of the brave women of old,
and examined, but did not eat the snails
which were presented for our delectation.
"Oh, Lord!" exclaimed our English
friend — by the way, he was a poet — as,
after many struggles, he drew out on his
fork a most untempting-looking morsel
from the shell, and waved it aloft for our
inspection. But our disgust changed into
curiosity when we heard the sound of
singing from the other table, and running
to the wide doorway, saw an old lady of
eighty, standing at the head of the table,
her beribboned lace cap a little askew, the
folds of her gray silk dress smoothed over

her ample figure, her cheeks rosy and her eyes shining with excitement, as she sang the Song of the Escalade. By this time the crackers had been pulled, and we were all decked in gay paper caps listening, smiling, to Madame.

> "For our dear country's glorious sake
> Your ancient valor now awake!
> Your praises never cease
> Of the valiant Genevese.
>
> "Of the days of the Escalade
> Long may the fame resound!
> Of the days of the Escalade
> Long live the cannon's sound!
>
> "And we who sing with hearts aflame
> The glory of our fathers' name,
> Oh, let us strive for aye
> To follow in their way!"

"L'Escalade! l'Escalade!" she sang at the end of each verse; and with a warlike gesture, she struck the big chocolate kettle a smart blow, and out poured a stream, not of boiling water, but of bonbons. It did remind one of the warlike women of old Geneva. "Just like 'em," maliciously remarked the poet. "Ah! but they did it to save the men they loved," I replied, which argument seemed to appeal to his poetic judgment.

And after that there was a dance, — a sailor's hornpipe, I believe; and then we all hurried out into the streets into a surging crowd of maskers, boys, girls, men, and women. In a whirl of carnival fun, with decorations and illuminations on every side, amidst musicians and stragglers from the procession, on we pushed with our stalwart guard, — sometimes dragged bodily around corners, or swept off our feet in the press of the crowd, — on over the Pont Mont Blanc, past the old clock-tower to the open square where the flower-market was held on Saturdays, where we stood for some time waiting for the procession. It came at last, with knights and plumes, torches and chariots, cars and music, and much tinsel and gold lace. Three hundred gentlemen of the first families in Geneva, I remember, were gorgeously dressed and magnificently mounted, and certainly presented a vision of beauty to their adoring families. "Home," as Mr. Pepys says, to mulled wine and biscuits by the fireside in our little salon, where the "marmites" came again into play, to hold the hot water, not this time to be poured upon devoted masculine heads, but to be mixed by the ladies in potations for their own trusted knights.

CERTOSA.

IT was a bright, clear, sunny afternoon when we drove from Florence over to Certosa. The monastery stands on a hill which is clothed with cypresses and olive-trees, and surrounded by other hills. Near here the two rivers, the Ema and the Greve, meet; and the pretty Ema, which gives its name to the valley, winds in three silver curves back of the monastery grounds. We had read that it was founded in 1341 by a Florentine, Niccolò Acciajuolo, who had amassed a fortune by trading in Naples, and that the fortunes of the Carthusians being decadent, there were only fifteen monks now living there. So we had expected ruin and desolation, and were surprised at the smiling, cultivated landscape that met our eyes, as we drove through the old arched gateway surmounted by a dilapidated figure of a saint. Winding up the hill past the olive-trees, the vines, the vegetable gardens, and the peach-trees in bloom, all so trim and well cared for, we concluded that the fifteen inmates were happy and prosperous.

Arrived at the turreted entrance-way to the church, we met a delightful white-bearded monk, like David, " of a ruddy countenance." We glanced approvingly at each other after a look at his clean, white gown and his nicely blacked shoes, and willingly followed him into the church, enjoying the rich, Tuscan accent of his English. Near the door, another white-robed monk was cleaning the stoup for the holy water; and we stopped to admire the lovely little carved angel figures, which, crossing their arms, support the marble basins. Our guide smiled, well pleased at our enthusiasm, and told us that the sculptures were not, as everything else seemed to be, of the "cinque cento," but of the "setto cento." How clean everything was! Cleanliness seemed to be the predominant rule of the order.

We crossed the floor of porphyry and marble to look at the cherub faces carved in oak on the choir stalls, and at the four statues of saints that stood behind the altar. Passing through a succession of chapels, each dedicated to a different saint, we paused to admire carved doors in arabesque designs, and tombs, one being a recumbent figure of a brother of the order, and pictures ascribed to Albertinelli, and went on to the cloisters, which are Spanish. The frescos, I think, were not remarkable; but our guide pointed to one of a brother pressing his finger on his lips to mean silence, and we lowered our voices as we passed the little graveyard,

OLD WELL, CERTOSA.

and noticed the violets growing at our feet, and the young brother drawing water at the old well in the centre. Taking our places in the *loggia*, which a party of English people vacated to make room for us, we caught a glimpse from the window of the country beyond. " Bella vista ! " our monk fervently exclaimed ; and we agreed, as we looked out at Fiesole directly opposite, and the river and olive hills below. Around the cloister were the little houses for the monks, each built separately, and each having a small window opening on the court, through which dinner is passed to the person inside.

That day, however, was a "festa," and dinner was to be eaten in the refectory. It was decorated with banners for the occasion; and on the high reading-desk was a vase of flowers. We turned to watch a brown-habited Franciscan, who was evidently being shown over the monastery by one of the brothers. His dark eyes, which he turned expressively upward, and his long nervous hands, which he clasped, unclasped, and then threw out in animated gestures, reminded us of the pictures of Saint Francis in the gallery, until an arch glance in our direction showed that his thoughts were not all turned heavenward. Was he, too, a *poseur* when foreign ladies looked admiration?

We lingered, fascinated by the picturesque glimpse of monasticism, until, mindful of our time, we moved on to the papal apartments and the Spezeria. Somewhat dreary was the salon devoted to the Pope's use when he visits the monastery; and shaky seemed the old bed on the pillows of which many papal heads have lain, and very insecure seemed the gilt crown suspended over it. Carved chairs were ranged stiffly along the walls of the antechamber, where hung mirrors and portraits of popes, most prominent, of course, being the thin, intellectual face of Pope Leo.

In the Spezeria were rows of pretty Faenza flagons of Chartreuse and perfumes. The famous liqueur is obtained by the distillation of various aromatic plants, — carnations, absinthium, and the young buds of the pine-tree, — and can be had in three degrees of strength, which are indicated by the colors, green, yellow, and white. Each bottle is stamped with the device of the order, — a globe surmounted by a cross. The Carthusian order was founded by Saint Bruno in 1084, and the general of the order is still the prior of the Grande Chartreuse, near Grenoble in France. Its distinguishing characteristics seem to be the cassock and cloak of very thick white cloth, the living each one in his separate dwelling, and a general respectability of deportment, which has gained for it the distinction of having been one of the few orders whose monasteries have never been subject to reformation of rules or morals. Eucalyptine, a tonic in cases of malaria, and a mineral salve are also made by the monks.

It took a long time to select our perfumes, for English ladies were buying too; and the dignified brother in charge was somewhat perplexed at our long indecision over mignonette or heliotrope, rose-geranium or violet. A mischievous twinkle in Egeria's eyes, as we passed through the gateway, warned me to look for something amusing; and our last view of the monastery included the brown figure of the handsome monk, standing with bent head in an attitude of humility.

The Duomo and Giotto's campanile were outlined clearly against the glowing sunset sky, as we drove out of the gate on the hill-top, and the soft, fragrant air blew refreshingly in our faces.

ITALY.

A RAINY MORNING AT SAN MARCO.

TOO rainy and dark a morning for the galleries, and our " gallery fever " had somewhat abated, so we voted for San Marco. When a travelling party only numbers two persons, not much time is lost in coming to a decision; although we were often so anxious each to please the other that our destiny was fixed by the aid of an American cent.

Heads that day meant San Marco; and heads it proved to be when I lifted the coin from the floor after some moments of anxious suspense.

There are no longer monks at San Marco; but in the church are always two or three Dominicans ready to act as guides. While we waited, shivering a little in the cold church, we noticed a monk, in crossing before the altar, carefully stoop to lift his clean white gown before genuflecting, with an expression that implied that, to him, dust was almost as abhorrent as impiety. The church seemed bare and plain to us, as did the monastery; but we had been reading the Life of Savonarola, and had seen in the Palazzo Vecchio the room where he had spent his last night, and the fine modern statue of the ruler monk. Our minds were filled with the memory of that strange, stern face, and with freshened interest we entered the prior's cell. Egeria seated herself for a moment in his armchair, which is anything but comfortable, — indeed, in that respect resembling our impressions of Calvin's and Shakespeare's chairs, and Napoleon's throne. One could well imagine the stern, enthusiastic prior sitting here at

SAVONAROLA'S CELL.

his desk, and writing some of the wonderful sermons which afterward convulsed Florence. We were shown his bust, some of his writings, his rosary, his hair-shirt, and a piece of wood from the pile on which he was burned. The frescos in the two inner cells were by Fra Bartolommeo, who gave up the world for love of Savonarola. At the dinner-table at our *pension* the day before, a German Fräulein announced the fact that three monks had just been burned in the Place Signoria. We were much startled, fearing that the Inquisition had recommenced in Italy, and if auto-da-fé's were to become common, would not Americans and heretics suffer too? After explanation, hindered by a confusion of languages, as the Fräulein spoke only French and German, we were relieved to find that the event had taken place three hundred years before, and that we had no occasion to dread the baleful fires of persecution in Florence.

In the chapter-house we sat a long time, studying the many figures in Fra Angelico's Crucifixion, the faces in which stand out so wonderfully, and reading Mrs. Jameson's description of what she calls a sublime and wonderful composition. I think even without her aid we should have appreciated "the pathetic beauty of the head of the penitent thief and the mingled fervor and intellectual refinement in the head of Saint Bernard." The framework of prophets and sibyls interested us greatly, having beneath Saint Dominic, from whom springs the tree of the order branching into many saints. Going upstairs, we saw the Angelico Madonna and Child, painted in the corridor, and in a cell his Annunciation.

Then, too, we visited the cell of the good Bishop Antonino, and communicating with it a cell inhabited for a time by Cosimo de' Medici. And glancing through the library, with its collection of illuminated and choral books, we escaped to our favorite monastic spot, the cloisters. Here, in early cloister life, Savonarola used to discourse under a damask-rose-tree to a knot of young brothers gathered about him; and one wishes that some of those early, poetical discourses had been preserved to us, that we might study more fully the wonderful monk whose impress is still left on the Florence of to-day.

FOUNTAIN OF NEPTUNE, BOBOLI GARDENS, FLORENCE.

A WEDDING AT OUR PENSION.

THE doorway of our *pension* in Florence was one day adorned with the motto "W. gli Sposi" enwreathed in ivy, which intimated a welcome to the man and maid who were that day to be united in the bonds of holy matrimony. The bride had passed her first youth, and the bridegroom was an elderly and amiable bachelor; but as our landlady had married four other daughters advantageously long before, and would still have left with her one who was sweet-mannered, and who, although a cripple, seemed the mainstay of the household, there was great rejoicing in the family over the unexpected event. The acquaintance had been a recent one, and the courtship brief. Evidently the bridegroom thought he had reached an age when time was precious; and the bride, for her part, had responded with alacrity, as a good salary in his profession of engineer made everything move to the tune of " Haste to the Wedding."

We had been somewhat inconvenienced by the preparations and the preoccupation of Madame, but with the other *pensionnaires* had yielded an indulgent acquiescence to the statement that all things give way to a wedding. "But why such elaborate costumes, music, and reception? It surely was not necessary at their age!" Well, why not? Must one be deprived of music, flowers, friendship, and festal gatherings because one is for — hush, we will not whisper how many years old! And when the *fiancée*, a sentimental expression overspreading her face, had confided to us that the wedding journey was to be a trip to Rome and Palermo, which cities she had never seen, and that her future husband, during his recent travels in the North, had seen snow for the first time, and in the exuberance of his feelings had fallen on his knees and kissed it, we sympathized at once, and only regretted that we could not be present at the ceremony. We could, however, peep into the long dining-room and see the masses of lovely flowers, the harps and other floral emblems, the branches of mimosa, and on the walls more ivy-wreathed mottoes,— " L'Amour fait l'union," "L'Union fait la force," " Dio benedica gli sposi,"—and the table set for a large family party.

We could also look out from our window, and from the altitude of the fourth story see the bride depart for the church, and a little later return with her *sposo;* and we could watch the arrival of the wedding guests.

Our midday meal was served in a small anteroom adjoining the large hall, and through the closed doors we could hear the bursts of laughter, the making of toasts, the chattering of the thirty children invited to the feast, and later the tinkling of the mandolins. Our repast, of course, was hurried and confused; and the married people present were incited to entertain us with long reminiscences of their own weddings, one elderly German gentleman, whose eyes glistened at the recollection, giving a long story of old-time marriage observances in Germany, while the bachelor of our party, a quiet, literary Frenchman, listened with a gentle, pitying expression. Feeling a little out of it all, as neither looking back upon matrimonial experiences or looking forward to anything of the kind just at present, we slipped away for our afternoon walk. Just as we passed the door of the salon, some one flung it open, and there stood the bride in her white dress and wreath, nodding and smiling to us; and a tall handsome Italian girl, who seemed to have been bridesmaid, came out in the hall, gracefully inclining her pretty head.

So, we congratulated ourselves, as we walked along by the Arno, we had really seen a great deal of the wedding. It was a clear, bright day in February, and the sun fell warmly down on the Lung Arno, and touched the curls of the little girl who ran toward us holding out bunches of violets; while her father stood,

PONTE VECCHIO, FLORENCE.

laughing, at the foot of Garibaldi's monument, beside his great basket of purple red, and white anemones, primavera, tulips, and white lilacs. Yes; we bought the violets, — for who could resist the little dimpled face?—and went on our way toward the Cascine, looking with delight at the purple light on the mountains and the olive-trees drawn like a silver veil across the landscape, and at the shallow, pebbly river flowing at our side. The Cascine was gay with carriages that afternoon, for the military band was to play, and the fashionable world of Florence had come to hear it. Cavalry officers caracoled about the coupés, which held beautifully dressed ladies and children; and bicyclists spun along toward the more secluded roads; and elderly gentlemen, mounted on roan horses, trotted calmly by. Beggars and flower-women and on-lookers crowded the paths bordered by myrtle and bay-bushes in flower, and sat on the wooden benches under the graceful, drooping branches of the cypress-trees. As we penetrated into the green depths of the woodland, we met a noble pair of milk-white oxen drawing a cumbrous wagon.

We returned to the *pension* to encounter the bridal party at the door bidding the bride good-by. The "bagaglio" seemed to be modest, consisting of a few cloth-covered hold-alls, and a leather hat-box. Friends and relatives crowded around, kissing noisily both bride and bridegroom, who started off gayly for the wedding-journey,— she in a long ulster and plain bonnet, and he in a new overcoat. "So," as some one expresses it, "they were wed, and I have not heard that she chided more than most."

But there was no sign of chiding when, a fortnight later, there was a family reception given by the mother in honor of the bride. This time we were invited, and sat for an hour in the circle that gathered around the bride, and listened to the mandolin-playing and singing of the bride's nieces, while in the opposite corner was formed a group of men playing chess with the bridegroom. Poor emotional Madame was in tears, as usual; but the daughter who had recently lost a scarcely regretted American husband, was cheerful in her crape, and played a piano accompaniment to the mandolins; the lame daughter, self-forgetful, smiled as brightly as ever; and the air of sober, subdued festivity that pervaded the room was in keeping with the age and circumstances of the newly married pair.

We sipped our wine and nibbled our cake, and smiled our congratulations at the dignified bride. We had sometimes called the salon gloomy, for the house, like all Florentine *pensions*, had once been a palace, and the high ceilings and faded frescos were anything but cheerful on dark days; but that evening the firelight, the guests, mountain-bred Dina passing the collation, — perhaps the unaccustomed presence of children, — made the old room for once really gay.

VILLA LIFE IN ALGIERS.

HEAD OF ARAB GIRL.

THE scent of a handful of eucalyptus seeds brings back to me a white villa on the heights of Mustapha Supérieur, with a large garden, the greater part of it white with irises and lilies, an avenue of eucalyptus-trees, and another avenue of flowering-almond-trees. In a sheltered nook in the garden were comfortable, worn wicker chairs, and a little iron table suggested sketching, letter-writing, and afternoon tea. On a roof-piazza, ladies strolling in the moonlight could see clearly defined the bay far below, and the outlines and lights of the harbor. From the window of one special little room one could look far, far off to the Metidja plain and the snow-capped Djurdjura Mountains. There was a little colony of ladies at the Villa des Olives, mostly Scotch and English; and the feminine serenity of our society was broken only by the coming of one representative of the sterner sex, who, being somewhat invalided, and moreover of studious tastes, did not prove a greatly disturbing element.

Formerly the house had been an Arab villa; and the yellow dome that marked the residence of a Marabout covered a curious octagonal bedroom and the Moorish arcaded courtyard, where a fountain should have played, but did not. The hallway floored with Moorish tiles was a reminder of Arab times; and somewhere, we did not know the exact spot, but fancied it was directly under the drawing-room alcove, the holy man himself was buried. We did not at all object to his being there. Indeed, as we sat there in the evening, playing Halma and Buried Cities, or listening to music, we rather liked to think of the Marabout and talk of him. We supposed that he had led a retired, meditative life, studying sacred books and sometimes walking in the garden with his disciples. Of course, a Marabout did not marry. Imagination could not therefore supply lovely Arab ladies smoking cigarettes, and drinking coffee by the plashing fountain. No, the worn tiles had not been worn away by the tripping of tiny slippered feet; and the roses climbing on the inner wall of the courtyard had never been pulled by little henna-stained fingers.

We wondered whether our Marabout had been filled with spiritual pride, or whether he was like the Arab teacher, Malek, who lived eight hundred years ago, and who, when forty questions were given to him one day, replied " I do not know " to thirty-eight of them. In recognition of this evidence of humility, he was made a Marabout, for, as his Moorish biographer adds, "only a man who cared more for God's glory than for his own, would have confessed to so much ignorance."

Egeria preferred the legend of Saint Geronimo, whose monument we had seen in the chief mosque, now the French cathedral. As an Arab child, he had fallen into Christian hands, had been baptized Geronimo, and as a young man, taken prisoner at Oran by Algerine pirates, and brought to Algiers in a pirate-ship, and steadfastly refusing to renounce his faith, was thrown alive into a block of molten concrete. The block may still be seen in the museum in Algiers; and the ardent young Arab Christian is memorialized in song and story as well as by the marble monument that confronts you as you enter the cathedral.

Studies of Arab life and the old piratical days beguiled the hours spent in the garden; and so exciting and intense became our interest that once, while absorbed in hearing a piratical tale of peculiarly blood-curdling quality, we started to our feet at the deep booming of cannon in the harbor. It was as if Lord Exmouth were again bombarding the town, or perhaps insurrectionary Arabs had gained possession of the fort and were firing on the French. Our perturbed nerves were only quieted by learning from Madame that the cannonading was only a salutation to the Russian fleet then in the harbor.

French lessons went on in the garden, and tennis-playing and flower-picking. Botany and entomology were full of interest, for in the field at the lower end of the grounds, near the Birmandries road, we gathered thirty-seven different kinds of wild-flowers, among them irises, crocuses, poppies, bugloss, mignonette, and great sprawling stalks of asphodel and fennel; and tiny white snails, horned beetles, and giant grasshoppers were found and carried indoors to be preserved as mementos. Then there were great fir-cones to be gathered for our drawing-room fire, eucalyptus leaves to be collected for a tea for the malarial patient, and orange blossoms and eucalyptus seeds to be dried for sachets. In the hedge that separated the vineyard from the carriage-drive, field mice ran in and out all day; and in April water wagtails, blue-headed jays, finches, and, later on, cuckoos and hoopoes sang, called, and flitted about over our heads. How noisy the cuckoos were, and how gorgeously plumaged were the hoopoes,

STREET IN OLD ALGIERS.

and how saucy was a certain little brown bird whose name we never learned, and who chattered away — chee, chee, chee — from morning till night! And in the evening, when the moonbeams fell in the courtyard, the nightingales sang their full-throated melody, the scent of the orange-blossoms was blown in stronger sweetness, the odor of Turkish tobacco lingered in the air, and a spirit of magic and poetry was abroad. Then it was a delight to stroll under the arcades and linger in the shadows, — a vivid delight to breathe and listen, to be and to enjoy, to know that near us throbbed and heaved the Mediterranean, and that the soft wind that passed sighing, yet caressingly, above our heads, would pass on until it reached the desert.

In the afternoons the coachman was always washing the carriages on the great stone platform near the doorway, and the Kabyle gardener was lying asleep under a tree, white and wan, for it was his fast of Rhamadan, and he neither ate, drank, nor smoked from sunrise until sunset. Often the courtyard was gay with the figures of Spaniards in Toreador costumes, who came selling laces, silks, and fans. Arabs came too, spreading out their rugs, embroideries, and jewelry on the ground, waiting patiently for hours for the chance of selling one burnous, or one ordinary haick, or even two turquoise-studded spoons. An Arab who won our special favor was one with a peculiarly interesting, melancholy face and gentle manners. A touch of green on the end of the hood of his ragged burnous signified that he was a descendant of the Prophet; and the dignified way in which he touched first his forehead, then his heart, before offering his hand to us, bore witness to a nobility of heart, in our opinion, that redeemed rags from vulgarity.

The villa-grounds comprised three acres of land, part of which was cultivated for vine-growing, and it was interesting to watch the young shoots sprouting up, budding and putting forth new leaves, day by day, until the vineyard stood green and upright and lusty above the rich, brown furrows, where at first had been only the bare stalks. As we watched the pruning, thoughts came to our minds of the illustrations the vine had offered to prophets and psalmists; and Hebrew poetry seemed more beautiful and more intelligible now that we stood on Eastern soil, where the vine put forth its branches, and the husbandman tended it much as in patriarchal days. The vine brought out of Egypt was planted here, too, for there are many Jews in Algiers; and at every turn of the road in driving or walking, we were reminded of Bible pictures. Biblical, too, were our frequent picnic-luncheons of bread and wine, symbol of substance and spirit, going back farther than Melchizedek and his mystical offering.

It is predicted that the vine will become the fortune of Algeria, the exportation of wine to France alone amounting to thirty-two million francs a year. Of course, there are good years and bad years, as much of the hot sirocco wind is not beneficial to men or vines, although I met people occasionally who said they enjoyed sirocco air.

The wine of the Château Hydra is well-known, as is that made at Staoueli, where there is a Trappist monastery. We did not go, voting the drive long and uninteresting, and being told that ladies are only admitted to the ante-room, where "even silence begs," for to the usual rules of poverty and obedience the Trappist order adds that of silence. But a party of our friends did go, and were impressed with the hospitality of the monks and the ex-

ALGERIAN ARAB HEAD.

cellence of the wines, the perfumes, and the eucalyptine, although they could not agree whether the principal dish at luncheon was composed of fish or flesh. The monastery stands on the site of a battlefield where the French were victorious over the Turks.

There had died, some time before we reached Algiers, Cardinal Lavigerie, — the French prelate who did so much for Algeria and the Arabs, and who had died saddened by his unfruitful efforts to obtain encouragement and help from the government at home in his plans for extending the work of the church and French rule in Africa. His picture was in all the shop windows; and we heard accounts of the pomp of the funeral procession, and the lying-in-state in the cathedral. A noble man, every one said, successful in instituting his order of White Fathers, wearing the Arab burnous as habit, and who, had his ambitious dreams been realized, would have added much to the name and fame of France in Africa.

Primate of Africa and Archbishop of Carthage and Algiers, Cardinal Lavigerie was buried in the tomb which he had built for himself under the altar of the cathedral dedicated to Saint Louis in Carthage and inscribed "Africæ Primas, nunc cinis." The son of an officer in the customs, he became professor in the Sorbonne at the age of twenty-nine. Seven years later, being sent on a mission to Syria, he became so much interested in the Moslems that in 1867 he gave up his see of Nancy to accept the archbishopric of Algiers, hoping to re-establish the African Church of Cyprian and Augustine. The Cardinal was one of the most picturesque figures of recent times, whether in his vigorous and eloquent crusade against the slave trade, or in humane work among the Arabs during the great famine, or in preaching martyrdom to his devoted band of White Fathers. On one occasion, attired in full canonicals, he marched boldly up into the mountain fastnesses of the unruly Kabyles, and explaining to them that Islamism had been forced upon their ancestors, called upon them to return to the ancient faith. He said he did not like controversy, because it prevented his working miracles.

Hearing of this remarkable man incited in us a desire one Sunday afternoon to drive to the church of Notre Dame d'Afrique, on the top of the Bou Zarea Hill, to hear the vesper service. It was a glorious day, and the streets were full of Russian sailors, as we drove through the town, and started along the steep road leading up the hill. The band was playing in the square, and there was some species of bull-fight going on under a tent. "While thee we seek, protecting Power," sang out Egeria on the clear air. She was always singing it, and sometimes I found it irritating. There were occasions when it was pleasant, and soothed me, like a lullaby; but at others it aroused evil passions in my breast. However, in driving up the Bou Zarea heights with the breeze blowing freshly from the ocean, the old hymn-tune, fraught with memories of home church-goings, was sweet to my ears. Notre Dame d'Afrique stands in a commanding position on the highest hill around Algiers, and is a handsome Byzantine church. After the singing of the vesper service, priests and choristers chanted in the open air a solemn service beside a pall-covered bier for the repose of the souls of sailors who have perished at sea, the only such service given in the world. Around the apse of the church runs the inscription, " Notre Dame d'Afrique, priez pour nous et pour les Musselmans!" Notre Dame d'Afrique is represented by the figure of a black Virgin, it being thought that the Arabs are more attracted by portraying the Greek teaching that either the Blessed Virgin's complexion had become black during her sojourn in Egypt, or that she was naturally of a dark skin, in fulfilment of the text from the Canticles, " I am black, but comely, O ye daughters of Jerusalem." So some of the old writers explain the blackness of the antique images.

On a neighboring hill rose the Casbah, the old fortress where the Dey had lived, and where he gave the representative of the French government the historic blow with a fan that resulted in the entire overthrow of Turkish rule and the occupation by the French in 1830. "A Dey of Algiers," said Egeria, as we were driving toward home, — " not a day, but weeks, months, years of Algiers for me!"

DONKEYS AND CAMELS.

THAT is to say, one camel and many donkeys. For truly our experience was only with one camel, although, in the matter of donkeys, we became acquainted with hordes of the good-natured little animals. There " were all sorts and conditions" of donkeys in Algiers, from the thin little Arab *bouros*, bestridden by dignified, ragged Arabs, to the pretty little caparisoned creature we saw one day trotting along the road on its way to some fair equestrienne, or the important one who one morning put his head through the church window and brayed an Amen to our Lenten sermon. Droves of donkeys, laden with panniers filled with earth and stones for mending the road, passed along

DONKEY AND BOY

our lane daily; twenty-nine donkeys toiled up and down the new road, dragging the heavy roller; donkey-chairs containing lady-visitors, or ladies who felt suddenly ill or faint from the hot sun, drove to our door; donkeys ridden by small English boys passed on the road to the Bois de Boulogne; and donkeys drawing the Arab stages jogged along the road to Birmandreis. What so soothing on a hot, sleepy afternoon as the distant braying of a donkey! How it mingles with the call of the hoopoe, and gently disposes one to sweet slumbers and sweeter dreams!

We spent much of our time in the garden. There, under the fir-trees, chatting of nothing in particular, and watching the Kabyle gardener at his work, we waited for the green lizards to come for their sunning on the old wall, and chose, among the anemones and violets and crocuses and irises, flowers for the adornment of the dinner-table. At such times, the occasional braying of the donkeys in the direction of the adjacent quarry and the answering call of Martin, who was tethered somewhere near the flowering-almond-trees, formed a pleasant interlude to the tum-ti-tum of the "Marseillaise," which was played on a *guimbori* by an Arab strolling along the lane. At sunset we often walked over to the quarry, where the wild mignonette grew luxuriantly over the fields beyond the rocks. At that hour many carriages might be met on the Birmandreis road, for it was a favorite drive among the English residents; but the donkeys had finished their day's work and had gone home.

This distant braying of donkeys might be pleasant; but pleasant we could not call the roaring that broke upon our affrighted ears one morning. Our first thought was of jackals. But had they really such powerful lungs? Looking from the window, we saw the camel which belonged to the town photographer, and was now standing in the garden roaring mightily. This animal was taken about for English and American ladies and gentlemen to taste the pleasure of camel-riding in short stretches up and down the road, or to indulge them in the sport of being photographed in Arab costume on camel-back, as if they had really made an expedition into the desert.

We, however, modestly limited our desires to a ride to the Bois and back. As it was a perilous joy, the gentlemen were to try it first; and the two Arab attendants induced the great, ungainly creature to kneel and allow two of our party to take their places on the sacks and cloths that formed the so-called saddle. We adjured them to hold tightly by the ropes, as they rode slowly by, the camel still uttering the sounds of terror which had first alarmed us, and reached the gate just in time to startle the horses of a returning carriage, and seriously frighten its occupant by the unexpected apparition. Two by two, we took our turns in riding the hungry, angry camel up and down the road, under the eucalyptus-trees. Assured by the evil-looking Arab attendant that although the "chameau" was wicked, yet he was old and could not injure us, — for was not he, the Arab, there to protect us? — what a feeling of suspense and quivering terror pervaded us when the "chameau" slowly unbent his triply-jointed hind-legs and rose to his full height; and oh, what paroxysms of tremulous laughter possessed us, as, groping for the ropes, we swayed back and forth in our uncertain saddle! With what a feeling of relief we slid at length into those friendly, if dirty, protecting Arab arms on our way to *terra firma*, and

ALGERIAN ARABS AND CAMEL.

how gayly afterward at *déjeûner* we discussed the fatigues and pleasures — above all, the pleasures — of camel-riding in the desert!

Any comparison between donkeys and camels results in favor of the donkeys. The camels are stupid and of ugly disposition, while the donkeys are intelligent and generally docile and amiable. How awkwardly and clumsily the camel planted his great soft feet on the ground! How nimble and sure-footed was our little Martin! Of a truth, we exclaimed, the expression "What a camel!" would apply far more suitably to a stupid human being than "What a donkey!"

In the lower town, on a back street near the bay, was a camel-yard, whence camels were sent out in caravans to the desert. While resting from their desert journeys, they often served as models for artists. Kneeling with their gay trappings under the shade of a friendly palm, they were sufficiently interesting subjects for innumerable sketches. Forty years seems to be the term of service beyond which they are rarely useful. Living or dead, they are of value, however; and after their long bondage, they are killed and their flesh is sold to the Arabs for food.

The John Bell Fountain.

AT THE JOHN BELL FOUNTAIN IN ALGIERS.

AT the fountain erected to the memory of Mr. John Bell, there was always a small force of Arab children who darted out upon unwary passers-by, demanding alms. In general, they were pretty children, with beautiful eyes and soft voices, and at first it seemed cruel to refuse them; but we soon learned that systematic denial was the only course to pursue if one wished to walk on down the hill alone and in quiet, for a few centimes insured an escort for the next half-mile.

One afternoon, having walked the four miles from Algiers, I sat down at the fountain to rest, and finding it for once deserted by Arab children and Arab cripples, could enjoy undisturbed the sight of the carriages passing by, filled with English and French villa-folk and driven by Arab coachmen in native costume. Here came wagon-loads of English tourists from the excursion-steamer stopping for some hours at Algiers, the turn-outs of the two doctors, one Swiss, the other English, who curiously resembled each other, the red-cloaked Spahis mounted on fine horses and passing always in a cloud of dust, and occasionally a lumbering old barouche containing a fat Arab gentleman and his three wives.

The fountain is of marble, and above the tablet dedicating it to the memory of Mr. Bell are Moorish tiles of such good design and color that with the aid of lead-pencil and tracing-paper we secured the outlines for embroidery. A road branches off to the right, leading down to the village of Mustapha Inférieur and the parade-ground of the French troops; and opposite is the plain building of the Hotel Kirsch, where the guests are sitting on the terraces smoking and chatting.

Just below the Kirsch are the extensive grounds of the Hotel St. George, built in the Moorish style and overlooking the Mustapha Bay, and farther down the hill is the English Library, where service is held on Sunday afternoons, and in which building resides and dispenses drugs the English chemist, — an important personage, whose views on the cholera question were eagerly sought after. Some distance below is the handsome front of the English Club. Rumors of afternoon dances, bachelors' balls, and masquerades at the club had penetrated even to the Villa des Olives, as had also tales of the meetings of the sketching club known as " The Portfolio."

But I am wandering away from the John Bell fountain, where I sat that afternoon in the sunshine, drinking in light and sound and color. On the white villas around me hung great magenta or copper-colored masses of the blossoms of the Bougainvillea, and the gardens were filled with roses, mignonette, and tall bushes of marguerites. It seemed difficult to believe that in America at this season were blizzards and snow-drifts.

Up the hill toward me came three negroes, fantastically dressed, and beating their tam-tams and playing on curious fiddles. They were the delight of the English children, and seemed honest and

good-natured, always grinning from ear
to ear. Following them went by French
officers in little open carriages, for the
Governor received that day at his summer
palace at Mustapha, where he had re-
mained since the preceding summer. The
ball which was generally given soon after
Easter at the summer palace, to the Arab
chiefs and dignitaries, would be omitted
this year, on account of the serious illness
of the Governor's child, but his Excellency
was at home to officers and civilians every
Thursday.

Among the carriages toiled patient
Biskrayans, the Algerian water-carriers
with their copper jars, and the Mozambites
in their coats of many colors, swarthy
Jews, all apparently well-to-do, industrious
Kabyles, their turbans wound about with
camels' hair cord, and stately Arabs riding
by on their donkeys. The Arab mode
of mounting always amused us, the invari-

able practice being to pull the donkey's head down and then climb up over his neck to a place, sitting sidewise, on the rope-tied cloth which served in lieu of a saddle. " O my ass! do not die yet; the spring will come and the trefoil will grow," says an Arab proverb; and the thin, wretched donkeys are withheld from dying by this consoling promise.

Another proverb says, " Words draw the nails from the heart," and it seems as if these silent Arabs might find relief in words from the oppression of their conquerors; for from all around the fountain seemed to go up the sigh of the Moor. We had seen the French soldiers behave with brutal insolence to Arabs, and others, grossly rude, push from the sidewalk a veiled Arab lady of the upper class, followed by her servant, carrying a basket of provisions on their return from market. We knew the intense sorrow and indigna-

ARAB AND DONKEY.

tion caused by the French arrogantly taking the chief mosque for a cathedral, and the lasting hatred felt toward the French generals who infringed the treaties made with the Arabs. There is always a certain sadness about a conquered people, and one cannot quite confound the industrious Kabyles, the hill people, or the warlike Arabs, the people of the plains, with the pirates and corsairs of the Turkish rulers and Spanish renegadoes. What wonder that the Arab rising in 1871 was nearly successful! What wonder that the Arab dislikes the French name, when he is certain of insult and contempt in the French courts of justice, in the market, and in every-day life!

> "Some things are of that nature as to make
> One's fancy chuckle
> While his heart doth ache."

And of this nature are all things pertaining to the Arab women. We had laughed at their baggy trousers, and had longed to know how many yards were swathed in folds about the poor things' legs, finding that twelve yards went to the making of each trouser-leg, and asking for the pattern. But when we saw their cramped, ungainly walk, their ugly stoop under the long folds of the *haick*, the shuffling of their slippered feet, the pathetic expression of their dark eyes above the stifling *yashmak*, and marked the thin forms covered by vest and sash, our hearts went out to them in pity. It took us some time to realize that they were our fellow-beings, and to become accustomed to their gliding motion, which was decidedly eerie at first. The English ladies who had come out to Algiers as medical missionaries said that they were gentle and tractable, very sweet in their manners, kind to their children, and grateful for care and attention. We wished that we might visit the interior of an Arab

ALGERIAN ARAB.

home and give some brief talks on dress reform, hygiene, and the higher education of women.

The day that we visited the Arab quarter, armed with branches of eucalyptus, — for the odors we encountered were not those of Araby the blest, — we peeped through an open doorway into an inner court, and saw standing on the upper gallery, leaning on the wooden banister, two or three Arab women without their veils, who, however, ran away at sight of us. It was late in the afternoon, and at the doors of the Arab cafés men were sitting on straw mats drinking coffee and playing cards. The little square shops were open to the air; and the loaves of bread spread out on the pans at the baker's looked so appetizing that we bought one loaf besprinkled with fennel-seed to carry away with us. A group of dignified men were sitting on rugs in one room with copies of the Koran before them. To one of them the gentleman with us gave an Arab translation of the New Testament, having learned the Arabic words for " This is a gift," and received in return a courteous bow and smile of thanks. The narrow irregular streets led up to the Casbah, and the fortress is now used as barracks by the French. In the throne-room is a chain suspended across from wall to wall, and from this chain used to be exposed the heads of the Christian and other slaves for twenty-four hours. The octagonal fort commands a wide view of the Mediterranean.

The most celebrated Moorish café is that outside of the Mustapha gate of the Jardin d'Essai, just beside a perfect Moorish fountain built some three hundred years ago, and which has often been a subject for the artist's brush. Here, if one is a man, one can stop for coffee, and *couscous;* but if one is a woman, one must pass by on the other side, and only look over to study the Moorish architecture and admire the effect of the trees hanging from the hill behind over the arched roof; or else revisit it in fancy, as I did that afternoon while sitting at the John Bell fountain.

INVALIDS, CHURCHES, AND CEMETERIES.

GROVE NEAR ALGIERS.

MY title sounds sombre enough, but no sequence was meant to be conveyed in the wording; for although the invalids visited the churches, they did not always end in the cemeteries. On the contrary, they seemed to improve from day to day,— one lady gaining twenty-one pounds in weight during her winter in

Algiers, another leaving entirely cured, and others improving so rapidly that we saw some of them at the theatre witnessing the representation of " Les Voyages de M. Perrichon," given by M. Coquelin and his troupe. The dainty humor and refined acting were probably more beneficial than repeated visits to the mosques, and M. Perrichon's two accounts of the adventure in the Swiss crevasse where *le petit sapin* saved or did not save his life, according to which lover he was speaking to, did more good, by provoking honest laughter, than the doctor's long-winded harangues. It is said that Algiers is a healthful, cheerful resort for the consumptive, for the dyspeptic, and for the hypochondriacal, nervous, and *ennuyé* of every degree. It was pleasant to see the improvement in the faces we encountered every day, to see ladies at first confined to their rooms able to drive about in donkey-chairs, and Russian princes recovering so far as to be able to dance and buy villas and Arabian horses; and clergymen's lungs growing strong enough to read Lenten services and deliver lengthy sermons.

At the Hotel Splendide, the invalids amused themselves with the young gazelle, the baby jackal, the parrot, and the monkey in the grounds, or stirred up the fat, green frogs in the fish-pond, where Monsieur Crapaud held undisputed sway, and hacked off with their penknives bits from the bark of the cork-tree. Occasionally the more venturesome of the invalids went out in sailing-boats to fish, with small results, in the Mediterranean; and sometimes they explored certain fearsome Arab lanes, where rocks and fallen trunks of trees and loose slippery stones obstructed the passage, and evil-intentioned Arabs were supposed to lurk in bands like unto those of the forty thieves. One day, finding ourselves without purses or watches, we started to walk through one of these lanes, and in a few moments were stopped by one of the Birmandreis gendarmes, who ran after us to urge us to desist from such a perilous undertaking, especially as we were unarmed; and he was distressed that he could not lend us his pistol, in view of possible breaking of the peace at Birmandreis.

But when the sirocco blew! Oh, that was indeed the ill wind that blew good to nobody. Then the nervous trembled, the consumptive coughed, the dyspeptic grew more savage in his denunciations of men and things, and the hypochondriac fell into a slough of despair from which nothing could rouse him. Pale faces flushed as in the heat of some deadly fever, and delicate lungs gasped for breath. Generally all invalids were rigorously kept indoors after four o'clock in the afternoon, the air after that being thought to be injurious.

Those who suffered from rheumatism, gout, and neuralgia went on to Hammam R'hira for the baths, where, although the bathing arrangements were far from luxurious, the properties of the hot springs are such that they who went crippled and depending on crutches for support returned straight and strong and rejoicing. The scenery there, of ravine and mountain and forest, is beautiful enough to give a welcome variety to people going from Algiers; and the proximity of big game in the pine woods near the plateau on which the hotel stands adds a touch of romance to the place. Some people even longed to hear the jackals howling in the night.

The English church of the Holy Trinity on the Rue d'Isly is Gothic, and interesting chiefly on account of the tablets which line the walls. The Easter service was made beautiful by the decoration of five hundred calla lilies and many palmettoes. Among the tablets the two most interesting are one erected in 1877 by citizens of the United States, associating the commemoration of their countrymen with the Jubilee of Queen Victoria, and another bearing the name of Commodore Decatur, the Bayard of our navy, and recording his capture of an Algerine frigate and brig in 1815, and his bombardment of Algiers. The Algerines having violated a former treaty with the United States, war had been declared; and Commodore Decatur gave the piratical defenders of Islam rule such a lesson that the Dey was glad to escape by paying an indemnity of sixty thousand dollars, and by signing a new treaty with the Americans, excluding all tribute. We held our heads higher, and a wave of loyalty swept over us, as we looked at the tablet that bore the name of

Decatur. We were ready with beating hearts to echo his famous toast, " My country, may she always be in the right, still, my country, right or wrong!" On the wall to the left of the pew where we sat that Easter morning was also a tablet telling the story of an English clergyman who was kept many years in captivity by the Moors, and who refused to accept his ransom when offered, preferring to remain with his hundred other Christian fellow-slaves than to leave Algiers free and alone.

At Mustapha Supérieur, at a sharp turn of the road and commanding a view of the bay, is a small granite Scotch church built by the late Sir Peter Coats. The Scotch minister comes for three months in the winter, and is then relieved by another arriving minister with his family to enjoy three months of agreeable life in North Africa. During the summer there are no English or Scotch services, and English residents who remain for the summer in Algiers if belonging to the low-church cult must spend their Sundays in solitary studies of the Bible, or if ritualistically disposed, may attend the vesper service at the little Roman Catholic church of Notre Dame at Mustapha. This was formerly an Arab house, and the Arab inscriptions and Moorish arches still remain. The decorations and hanging lamps are in keeping with the Arab building, and the tiny little house is filled with incense, and the Psalter is chanted inside the walls where verses of the Koran may still be read. So small is the little church that two very young boys had been selected for acolytes; and they and the tall priest in his red vestment quite filled the chancel, while the congregation was composed of Little Sisters of the Poor, with a flock of children, one French officer and his wife, and two old women.

As to the mosques, there are several. We had watched the Arabs performing their scrupulous ablutions in the mosque of the Place du Government, and one day we

MOSQUE, ALGIERS.

continued up a narrow street to find the oldest Arab temple in Algiers. From the glare of the street it was a relief to find ourselves in the cool, dim interior; and the clean matting and the whiteness of the walls were agreeable rather than otherwise. According to rule, we took off our shoes just inside the door, and walked down the long lane of matting, not I fear with native grace, but rather with the American shrinking from pins and tacks that are always supposed to be lying about loose on the floor at home, and proceeded to what looked like an interesting Mohammedan convocation. Grouped in Turkish fashion on the ground, were fifty or more elderly Arabs looking the personification of wisdom. Why is it they look so wise? Perhaps there is some subtle connection between wisdom and tobacco, and to "think and smoke tobacco," whether in whorls of cigarette-smoke or in denser clouds from *chibouk* or *hookah*, lends in time an astute expression to the countenance. For certain it is that whether in the mosque gathered in holy conclave, or in the bazaar of Mustapha Ben Aberrahman, the same unfathomable look of deep thought rested on the Moorish faces.

Perhaps there had been some reading or exposition of sacred books or discussion of ecclesiastical law before our entrance, or perhaps the Cadi had been called outside to settle some quarrel in the street, or interview some functionary who wished to divorce one of his wives, for at the moment of our approach a solemn stillness brooded over the Assembly. They seemed quite indifferent to the presence of Frankish ladies, and did not notice the attentions we paid to the beautiful children gathered in a group at the foot of a pillar or playing near the fountain. A soft, beautiful Mohammedan green was the color chosen most frequently for the dress of these noble, moon-faced boys, whose black eyes stared at us with a fire and intensity that a poet might envy.

This, the gathering in the mosque, was the place to see the men; but to see the Arab women unveiled, it was necessary to

ARAB GENTLEMAN.

go to the cemetery on a Friday afternoon. A man might have the privilege of visiting the Cafés Maures, but when it came to seeing the cemetery, then femininity stood one in good stead.

The English cemetery is on the heights of Mustapha Supérieur, on the edge of the hill overlooking the blue water, and there is no more peaceful or lovely spot in Algiers. The road there from the Villa des Olives was a favorite walk of ours. First you passed through the swing-gate, then down the shady lane into the road, which turned abruptly to the left after passing a large villa, then skirted along the edge of the cliff, past a rose-colored little house where a woman inside was always singing operatic airs, and two or three goats were always browsing outside. Frequently droves of donkeys were to be encountered on this road; but few pedestrians were to be met with, and you gained the quiet of the cemetery in a fit frame of mind to seek out the graves of the English, mostly young, who had looked their last on earthly scenes at Algiers. And fairer scenes for such last, lingering looks, and softer air for the final trembling, sighing breath can nowhere be found. The French division is ugly in its beaded decorations, heavy iron railings, and mottoes speaking of eternal regrets. But the English part is as sweetly simple as a country churchyard in England; and although the lych-gate is wanting, yet the crosses, the flowers, the tombs, the English names, all breathe the quiet content, the sunny cheerfulness, that make a graveyard in England something that, once seen, is never forgotten. You are almost tempted to wish to rest here, away from life's troubles and on the shore of the throbbing Mediterranean.

Still, one who loved English ways and

was loved in return by English people has said, —

> " But life is sweet, though all that makes it sweet
> Lessen like sound of friends' departing feet,
> And Death is beautiful as feet of friend
> Coming with welcome at our journey's end;
> For me Fate gave, whate'er she else denied,
> A nature sloping to the southern side;
> I thank her for it."

And one who has by birth, or who has acquired in some way, a nature sloping to the southern side will gain, in an hour spent in this Algerian cemetery, heart to face once more the rigors and rough weathers of life.

The Moorish cemetery is on lower ground and nearer the water. On Fridays the Arab women take the children for a day or half a day in the cemetery. Once inside the high wall that surrounds the enclosure, the *haick* is laid aside, — and even little girls of ten are shrouded in *haicks*,— and the Arab ladies, attired in their best raiment, stroll about the paths, visit the tombs of Marabouts, and eat their lunch under the shade of the palm-trees. Collected in groups, and seated on the ground around the graves, they recount in loud tones all the domestic occurrences of the preceding week, so that the spirits of the dead may keep up from week to week with the happenings in their families. They thus really spend the day with their dead. I hope that the family gossip so chatted over only records the pleasant bits of home life, and that family jars and worries and household disasters are not once mentioned.

Old women go about the paths selling long strips of candied stuff and sweetmeats to the children. Frightful old negresses lurk in shady avenues, and occasionally a Marabout is to be seen prostrate on the ground behind a tomb. Inside the high domed tombs are green earthenware lamps which resemble high candlesticks, but in reality have a bowl for holding oil; but they are seldom lighted, and there is little care bestowed on the cemetery. The children follow foreign ladies, begging for centimes and pulling their dresses with sticky fingers. English husbands and carriages must wait outside the gate for the ladies who have taken into their heads the vagary of paying a visit here. This is the only holiday in the week for the Arab women, and they meet their friends and enjoy one day of pure fresh air. There, too, they meditate on the day when they shall be taken from family cares and joys by " the separator of companions and the finisher of delights."

IN GOLF-LAND.

WHEN a lady in London told me that I should find a great many golfers in Aldeburgh, I wondered what she meant. Afterward I concluded that I had mistaken the sound, and that she had really said " gaffers ; " and as that is a good old English word, and our great desire was to see English village life, I was pleased to think that we should find gaffers at Aldeburgh. But once arrived there and established at the Brudenell Hotel, we learned that there were both gaffers and " goffers." The old English word was " goffers," and the modern word is pronounced as it was originally written. On the street that ran parallel to the ocean were to be seen old sailors sitting by the hour in the sun and talking

ENGLISH COTTAGE.

over the Lowestoft trade in salted herrings and kippers; and on the same street gentlemen in pony-carts drove leisurely along, holding long square-cornered canvas bags containing golf-clubs, the number of clubs corresponding to the skill of the player. The ancient and honorable game of golf was once played by Scottish kings on royal demesnes inside palace enclosures; and Robert Bruce and Wallace were no doubt conversant with niblicks and drivers, irons and brasseys, putters and tees, and drove their balls over furze bushes and ruts, and swept them smoothly over the putting-green as vigorously as any Parliamentary golfer of to-day. For it is a favorite recreation to-day with members of Parliament; and the Premier is evidently of opinion that two or three rounds a day on a four-mile golf course are good stimulants to nerves and brains overtaxed by long debates and obstructed bills on Welsh and Irish questions.

We wanted to know just what the ancient game was, so I looked it up in Strutt's book of Sports and Pastimes, and found that "goff, or bandy-ball" was played early in the fourteenth century, as is shown by an illuminated manuscript book of prayers of that period which contains a picture of two persons playing golf. In Mr. Strutt's illustration, the two chubby little figures seem but mildly interested in the sport. One swings his club in an angle which is not the correct thing nowadays; and the other expostulates, whether at unfair play or at bad swinging, is left for the reader to decide. There is also given an historical anecdote related of Prince Henry, eldest son to James the First. "At another time playing at goff, a play not unlike to Pale-Maille, whilst his schoolmaster stood talking to another, and marked not his highness warning him to stand farther off, the Prince, thinking he had gone aside, lifted up his goff-club to strike the ball; meantyme, one standing by said to him, ' Beware that you hit not Master Newton,' wherewith drawing back his hand, he said, ' Had I done so, I had but paid my debts.'"

Aldeburgh, in East Suffolk, on the coast of the German Ocean, boasts of golf-links that are four miles in extent; that is, in playing a game, one walks over four miles of ground, from hole number one to hole number eighteen. There are links at Yarmouth and, I think, at Lowestoft, and all that part of the country is noted among fishermen for the broads, — great shallow tracts of water, lying here and there as if carelessly dropped from heaven, — and among sportsmen for the golf-links, which are among the best in England. Those in Aldeburgh are situated on high ground on the road to Saxmundham, beyond the railway station. The ground is covered with gorse bushes; and in many places are holes made by the wild rabbits, treacherous hiding-places for balls, and under the bushes are the nests of the meadow-larks, who sing here all day long as we never had heard them sing before. The little club-house, where you can obtain tea, whiskey, beer, bread, and cheese when hungry, is flanked by a tiny workshop where clubs are constructed. The sweet fresh air blowing down through the pine woods is peculiarly soothing, and if the players are ever overcome with drowsiness, — as we were after an hour or two of walking, — we should not have been surprised to see them drop down and yield to sleep, on the ground near the furze bushes, or on the beach under shelter of an upturned boat.

On the way back to the beach the road passes the village church of St. Peter and St. Paul. The tower and archway are the

AN ENGLISH GIRL.

best parts of the church, and there are remains of curious carvings in the poppy-heads which adorn some of the benches. The church is built of stone and flints. There are some interesting old tombstones in the graveyard, and the peal of bells is very sweet-toned. On the royal wedding-day the bells rang marriage-peals all day long, and made cheerful music to unaccustomed American ears; and, again, when a daughter of one of the fishermen was married, the bells rang out and the flags flaunted across the village street just as they had done for the wedding of the Princess. I think the Church is firmly established at Aldeburgh, and there is little dissent to contend with. We noticed two modest little chapels belonging respectively to the Primitive Methodists and to the Plymouth Brethren; and we learned that among the two thousand inhabitants there was one Roman Catholic, who by reason of his faith was very unpopular among the sturdy Suffolk people. We early became accustomed to the dialect, and understood that in polite Suffolk, "loydy" meant lady, and "tayble" stood for table, and "ee got 't hat on" translates into "he has got on his hat." But, unfortunately, when we wished to ask a farmer for permission to cross his fields, or stopped a rustic maiden in a narrow lane to inquire our way, both maid and farmer would reply in English as good as our own; and we would disappointedly sigh, "Ah! but we hoped to hear real Suffolk." Still, there are many people who speak dialect at Aldeburgh.

The cottages of the fishermen all have names, — "Providence Cot," "Contentment Villa," or something else equally suited to rural life, — and in every window stand pots of geraniums.

The beach is a pebbly one, and bathing is considered somewhat dangerous, although

RUSTIC MAIDEN.

during six or eight weeks in the summer bathing-machines are drawn up in a row, and the bathing-masters do a lively business for an hour or two each day. The lifeboat is always on the beach, and coastguardsmen are constantly seen. At the farthest northern point is the village of Thorpe, where the Lord of the Manor lives; and near the White Lion Hotel is the old Moot House, or town hall, an Elizabethan building with latticed windows, tall chimneys, and much interesting ornamentation on the woodwork. Here one day we were shown the old records, deeds dating from the time of Philip and Mary and of Edward the Sixth, and papers relating to trials of smugglers.

The northern end of the beach is called Slaughden, and has docks and boats on the river Alde. Across the river is the Martello tower. Although to-day more picturesque than formidable, the tower was built in preparation for the expected assaults of an invading army under Napoleon Buonaparte. Occasionally we rowed down the river to Orford, where are a fine church and the remains of a castle. As the mudbanks extend far into the middle of the river and the current is strong, the pull home was always pretty tiring. Once, when Egeria was in London, I went to see an English circus, and on another occasion went with the same party of people on an afternoon excursion down the river Orwell, through the country that Constable painted, to Felixstowe and Ipswich, the site of Cardinal Wolsey's house. Aldeburgh is not without her notabilities, for here the poet George Crabbe was born, in 1754.

I must not forget to speak of our long drives over the commons to fine ruined abbeys, old churches, or gentlemen's places, *not* to attend a political meeting, — for I could not get Egeria interested in the Liberal party, the Home Rule Bill, or the House of Lords, although I am sure that Billy the pony would have trotted toward the white tents of the Liberal orators as willingly as he trotted twenty-five or thirty miles in other directions. Neither must I forget the lapidary's, where we inspected the clear stones and amber picked up on the beach in the autumn, nor the stationer's, where we bought the Parish Magazine, nor the pastry cook's, where we bought penny buns, nor the library, where we used to sit at the open window, looking over the illustrated papers and breathing in the sea air, and the perfume of the sweet-peas and mignonette that was wafted in from the beds below. The hawthorn was in flower when we first reached Aldeburgh in May, and the broom — the Plantagenet flower — flamed in golden yellow over the moors, and then paled again into nothingness before we left. And sitting one day, half dreaming, in the flowery sunshine, the following fancy came into my mind.

A TWOSOME AT GOLF.

THE golf-links were quite deserted. One reason for this was that it was Monday, and the people of Aldeburgh seldom play golf on Monday. Moreover, it was moonlight, and the people of Aldeburgh, although enthusiastic golfers, never play by moonlight, So, as I said, the field was clear.

Down on the beach near the Moot House, the waves were glistering with phosphorus, and lumps of amber lay among the pebbles. But who cared for phosphorus or amber when the path of the moonglade led directly over the sand-pit to where the red flag of hole number five fluttered lightly in the breeze.

"Jack," whispered Tim, "are you for a game?"

"Ay," returned Jack, cautiously; "where are those rascals of caddies?"

"I ordered them to be here at eleven," said Tim. "They won't earn their gorse-money at this rate. There they come flying round the corner, carrying the clubs in their beaks. I have the balls safely hidden in a hole here, for fear they should get broken."

Balls broken, caddies flying and carrying the clubs in their beaks? But I must explain. Jack and Tim were two wild rabbits who lived on the moors near by; the caddies were four little wild partridges; the clubs were branches broken from the whyn bushes; and the balls? Well, the balls, I grieve to say, were eggs stolen from the nests of the meadow-larks. The club-house lay black in the shadow, for Mrs. Hawthorn, the jolly old care-taker, was asleep and snoring an hour since, and Carrick, the professional, was down in the town watching a game of billiards at the window of the White Bull. The dewdrops sparkled on the grass of the moor, and the wind passed through the branches of the pine-trees in the wood, and blew gently over the commons laden with the scent of the broom. The red flags beckoned enticingly in the moonlight.

"Never felt so frisky in my life," said Tim; and he turned a somersault while his caddy number one made the tee, and caddy number two flew on to watch where the ball should go.

"Those tree-toads are making a dreadful row. A fellow can't hear himself think!" said Jack; and he rose on his hind-legs and buttoned the brass buttons of his scarlet jacket before taking a magnificent swing with his club.

"Dinna hurry the swing; keep your ee on the ba'," shouted back Tim, as he scampered on after his caddies.

"Hi, hi! you're in the sand-pit, and lose two if you take the ball out!" called Tim, a little later.

What a jolly game it was, what unnecessary frisks and gambols and détours on the part of Tim and Jack; what little cries of excitement on the part of the caddies! How vigorously the clubs were swung, and how lightly the white balls were sent skimming through the air! The stupid bats, wheeling overhead, were quite bewildered; and the big, buzzing brown insects got a smart slap of the paw for getting in the way. The meadow larks stirred uneasily in their sleep, and then nestled down more snugly in their nests as the gamesters passed them. Already they had passed the eighth hole, and had crossed the ruts on the road to the ninth, when Tim exclaimed, "Hi! dash my luck, where did my ball go?"

"Here, sir, here," breathlessly chirped the caddies, fluttering on to the mouth of a black little hole in the ground. "Here, Mr. Speckle-back, give us our ball, please!"

"What do 'ee want at this hour o' 't night? Barring loydies, I don't turn out for 't anybody," grumbled in sleepy broad Suffolk the toad in the hole.

Here was a dilemma. No entreaties could stir him. The ill-natured old fellow was too lazy to move, and finally Tim cried, "Never mind! Count that ball lost. I have plenty more in my pockets. Play from outside the hole." And on went the game as madly and merrily as before. In no time they were putting for the last hole.

"Ha! ha! I've won the monthly medal,"

shouted Jack, neatly sending his ball into hole number eighteen.

"Rum, tum, tiddledy yum, who's for a drink with me?" sang Tim, as he raced off to the brook.

And the game of golf was ended.

OXFORD AND CHERWELL RIVER.

WITH THE DONS IN OXFORD.

WHEN we told our landlady in Oxford that we were Americans, she objected that we spoke very good English. We assured her that we always tried to speak good English; and after one searching glance that seemed to read us through and through, she accepted our credentials and allowed us to take possession of the sitting-room and two bedrooms on the third floor which in term time were occupied by two undergraduates. The photograph of one of them, a student at Brasenose, adorned the mantel-shelf; and a cap and gown were rolled together on one of the book-shelves. It was August, and it was what the people of Oxford call the "long vac," and the heat was almost tropical. After a day or two's experience of it, we decided to remain quietly in King Edward Street until the advent of cooler weather for excursions and sight-seeing. One hot morning was beguiled by reading aloud Plato's Defence of Socrates; and I should like the undergraduate of Brasenose to know how much we enjoyed it, and how grateful we felt to him for having left it on the bookshelves.

From our window we could see the trams passing on High Street,— a few clergymen and brown, vested nurses from the Memorial Nursing Home being sprinkled among the working-people who sought a favoring breeze in a seat on the top of the tram. Looking in the other direction, we could see the end of King Edward Street, where it curved around to the entrance to the quadrangle of Oriel College, near where were lodgings whither we had been sent by friends. But the landlady had closed her house and gone away for the vacation, too; and William of Oriel, the bull-dog to whom we had been recommended, was also away, and his photographs with and without academic costume were to be seen in the windows of the shops on High Street.

As we turned from King Edward Street into the High, a few steps brought us to the architectural gem of that street of wondrous architecture, the Church of St. Mary the Virgin. Some one has

called it the most perfect example of
Gothic architecture in the world. The
old dame who showed us through the

AN OXFORD DON.

church told us of the University sermons
that are preached here. From her description we tried to picture the scene, —
the ladies in the gallery, the crowd of undergraduates surging below, the dons and

doctors in their colored gowns, and before the sermon the solemn words of the Bidding Prayer, the thanksgiving for the liberality of the Founders and Benefactors, floating through the crowd of young men who to-day enjoy the privileges conferred by these bygone worthies. Among the long list of names are those of Humphrey, Duke of Gloucester, Queen Elizabeth, and Archbishop Laud; and to one who joins in a hearty Amen to such a prayer, the repetition of these names must bring the benefactors of Oxford very near, almost in bodily presence. There is a mediæval flavor about the idea of praying for the souls of — but hush! that is Romish, is it not? and we must none of it; for we are standing in the Church of St. Mary the Virgin, where, for entertaining such sentiments, John Henry Newman deemed it wise to relinquish his fifteen years' vicarship, and to proceed to the charge at Littlemore, afterward to advance, with his apology for so doing, into the bosom of the Holy Roman Church. I wonder whether it was a thought of the serene figures of the Virgin and Child that surmount this porch, and the open book below, bearing the inscription "The Lord is my Light," that suggested the verses "Lead, Kindly Light" to the Christian mystic. When we saw the Virgin Porch, the vines of the Virginia creeper that overhang and enshroud it were already touched by the hand of autumn, and from the red-leaved mass of foliage rose the majestic figures. of Mother and Child, with an air of majesty and sovereignty that seemed to dominate all surrounding objects. As the sunshine rested on the stone faces, a ray of spiritual light seemed to illuminate the smile of the Holy Child and the steadfast gaze of His Mother. She is there a queen, for the porch is Renaissance of a severe and beautiful style, and the twisted columns and minor ornamentation are free from over-elaboration. It was erected in 1637; and at the trial of Archbishop Laud the building of this porch formed one of the items of his impeachment, although the real transgressor was his chaplain, Dr. Morgan Owen. The church was founded early in the thirteenth century, and, falling into a ruinous condition, was restored in 1492.

The College of St. Mary the Virgin, as Oriel College was first called, was founded about this time too; and De Brome, the first provost, was also Vicar of St. Mary's Church. So, as we walked through the quadrangle with an English friend, we connected the church we had just left with the college before us, and over the entrance we found a small statue of the Virgin and Child. The present buildings, our friend said, were ascribed to Inigo Jones; and she pointed out to us the windows of the rooms once occupied by Newman, Pusey, and Keble. The quad was peaceful that morning, and deserted save by one or two workmen who crossed the court on their way to and from the building, where some repairs were going on. Some flowering shrubs were in bloom under the pointed windows of the hall; and in the hush and heat of that August morning the buildings looked homelike and attractive. We were refused admittance because of the repairs going on, so we found our way, as we had often done before, to Magdalen Gardens and Addison's Walk.

There were several people sitting under the trees reading and sketching, and they looked up at us with interest as we passed them on the broad walk. Magdalen Tower is noble, viewed from every direction; and we wandered back and forth in the gardens getting different points of view, and comparing the engraving which we had been studying in a window on High Street — Holman Hunt's picture of the choristers singing the May Morning Hymn on the tower — with the actual building before us.

The deer in the grove were languid from the heat, and did not move at our approach. On we strolled, past the glory of color and bloom in the gardens, to the water-walks. The stream is so narrow that we could hardly call it the Cherwell River, yet river it is; and as we sat resting on the wooden bench overlooking the water, more than one canoe, propelled by an energetic English girl, glided noiselessly along at our side. Calm and strong and capable of more muscular work than lazily paddling a canoe did those English girls look, their

AN ENGLISH GIRL.

sailor-hats tilted down over their noses, and their linen blouses all made on the same pattern. They looked at us immovably as they passed, and a few moments later were lost to view under the arching branches of the trees that line the river-banks. It was unfortunate, our friend said, that we had not come to Oxford a week earlier. Then we should have been in time to see St. Giles's Fair, when St. Giles's Street is given up to country people, booths, and merry-go-rounds. We had had a surfeit of such fairs on the Continent, and were not eager for more; but we did regret not having seen the convention and festival of trained nurses over which Princess Christian had presided. The quadrangle of one of the colleges had been billowy for one afternoon with brown, black, blue, and gray gowns and veils, and white fluttering ribbons. It must have been a pleasure to meet thus at Oxford for the space of a summer day, called there by the mandate of the gracious lady who interests herself in all work for the sick and suffering.

We could not seclude ourselves much longer, for the allotted time of our stay in Oxford was drawing to a close, and Keble College called loudly for a visit. It was a long walk in the heat from King Edward Street; and we became somewhat irate by reason of various misdirections given us by unkind persons along our route. Unlike the other colleges, which have all been touched by the mordant tooth of time, Keble's is a new foundation, dating from 1870; and chapel hall and quad looked to us American rather than English, from their freshness. In the library we lingered a long time before Holman Hunt's picture, "The Light of the World,"— another reading of the University motto, "The Lord is my Light." In the hall we found a portrait of John Keble, M. A., Corpus Christi College, Professor of Poetry, Rector of Hursley, Hants, and author of "The Christian Year," and found much to admire in the sweetness of the curves of the lips and in the thoughtful brow. The chapel is rich in Venetian mosaic, which depicts scenes from both Old and New Testament history. The walls are lined with mosaic work, and the vaulted ceiling is supported by shafts of dark marble. A good time to visit the University, we thought, when dons and undergraduates are all away, and cleaning and reparation the only work done in the hall and study. The University Extension students were in Cambridge that August, on account of this same repairing in the New Schools, so there were no bands of intellectual ladies or groups of ambitious workingmen about the streets. The solitude was unbroken.

The cab-stand near the Martyrs' Memorial presented a depressed appearance, and the cabbies, napping in the sun, formed a picture of the unemployed; for often as we passed that way, and on the many occasions we stopped to study more closely our favorite figures of Ridley, Cranmer, and Latimer, never once did we see any one engaging a cab. There were no tourists, or at any rate no carriage tourists, in Oxford. We had the town to ourselves. For this occasion it was well for us that it was so; but we agreed that we would come again somehow, somewhen, for Commemoration Day and the boat-races.

The mention of boat-races brought the river to our minds, and ideas of excursions on the Thames. There was a flower-show at Abingdon one day; but the boats

THE WORKER AND THE CRICKETER.

would be too crowded, our landlady said, and the day was too oppressive, we said. Inaction and Rhoda Broughton sufficed for that day. And a proper choice Rhoda Broughton proved; for her home is in Oxford, and her lighter vein suited our mood that day as Socrates had done on a former occasion.

But the sun rose on a morning when we deemed it agreeable as well as expedient to spend that afternoon on the water. Our friend decided for us that Nuneham would be a delightful spot to picnic, so we arranged for an eight o'clock supper on our return, and packed our baskets, not so frugally as Mrs. Gilpin did hers, but with generous provision for a sudden access of hunger at tea-time; for hot weather makes one very hungry. If I remember rightly, it was just at three o'clock that we took the boat and passed the college barges on our way out into the stream. There were not many persons on board, so we found places on the shady side, and prepared ourselves to enjoy the scenery. There were two Americans on the boat, so there were a few tourists in Oxford, after all. These landed at Iffley to visit the little Norman church. The church looked so interesting that we regretted that we had not time to stop. An hour's trip brought us to Nuneham; and we stepped ashore in a fairy-like little bay, where there were swans floating on the water. Not far from the bank was the little tea-house, where picnic parties were already assembling. Scarcely glancing at the beautiful park in which we were, or at the magnificent oaks and elms above our heads, we hastened to secure a table to ourselves, to order tea, and to open our baskets. There we sat for I know not how long, eking out our repast with that "just one more" which is fatal to affectations of delicate appetites. Valiant trencher dames of Elizabethan mettle we proved ourselves that afternoon; and our quiet hour or two spent under the oaks of the park gave us time to compare our impressions of Oxford, and to question whether we had been even a little enlightened by our stay.

IZAAK WALTON'S COUNTRY.

THE corner of England watered by the Wye, the Trent, the Dove, and the Derwent may be rightly called the country of Izaak Walton, for through its dales and along the banks of its streams he wandered, rod in hand, finding not only material for his treatise on fishing, but health, contentment, and a quiet mind. It was with no special thought, however, of the English fisherman that we turned our faces toward Buxton for a month of Derbyshire air; it was rather with the idea that we should be only thirty-one miles from the town of Derby and its celebrated potteries. We promised ourselves that we would travel those thirty-one miles some market-day, in hopes of picking up some of the odd pieces of porcelain which are thrown out from the factories and find their way to the market-place, where cream-pitchers, sugar-bowls, and teapots of old-fashioned form are eagerly bought by housekeeping ladies. Our promise, however, was doomed to remain unfulfilled.

Buxton, lying in a deep valley, is divided into the old and new town; and it was in the new town, near the churches, shops, and bathing-houses, that we found our " Hydro " situated. For we had elected to stay at a hydropathic establishment, not for treatment, but for pleasant company and more homelike surroundings than a hotel could afford. Just in front of the house were the " slopes,"—a little patch of green hillside between two streets. Here on the benches persons were sitting all day, for the air there was pronounced by the doctors to be the most salubrious in Buxton ; and just below were the springs and the gardens, where the band played loudly enough for its music to be enjoyed on the slopes. St. Anne's Well has two saline springs, — one hot, the other cold, — which rise within a few inches of each other. In another pump-room is water from a chalybeate spring; and as this was considered efficacious for the eyes, people were continually crowding there with curiously shaped little glasses to drop the water into the eyes. The baths were curative in cases of gout and rheumatism, and the shop-windows are filled with stockings and undergarments of natural wool which are recommended for rheumatic patients. Crosses, jewelry, and ornaments of fluorspar and alabaster, together with strings of amber beads, are displayed as an offset to photographs and guide-books to this region.

The gardens are more attractive than shops or pump-rooms, for the grounds are laid out with much taste in landscape gardening. There is a diversity of water and land; and within the limits are a bowling-green, croquet-grounds, and lawn-tennis courts, a summer theatre, and a concert-hall where the band plays in wet weather. Nearly all Buxton is owned by the Duke of Devonshire, one of the richest dukes in England, and he was expected to be present in person at the opening of the horse-show in the autumn. While prisoner in the keeping of the Earl of Shrewsbury, Mary Stuart spent a short time in Buxton. There are shown the remains of an old hall; another record of her visit being found in Poole's Cavern, where among the curious stalactites illuminated daily by electricity is one called the Queen of Scots pillar. Perhaps it was some impalpable suggestion of this fact that hovered in the brain of our London hairdresser when he gave Egeria his views on " The Queen and her stalactites." Perhaps in the views of more advanced political thinkers in England, some of the statesmen who surround the Queen seem more like stalactites than satellites; but on the part of our hair-dresser, we concluded the word to be only a delightful slip of the tongue.

There are a number of hotels in Buxton, two of them being in the Crescent building, where the pump-rooms are; but as we had no acquaintances at any of them, we allowed ourselves to be entertained by the concerts, theatricals, and games which were provided for the amusement of the guests at the Hydro.

We found spiritual instruction in the Sunday services at St. Anne's little ritualistic church, and took our exercise in long walks to Solomon's Temple and the adjacent hills, and drives to the Cat and Fiddle.

For friends had joined us; and we, playing the part of hosts, had arranged for a series of excursions on the brakes that went daily in different directions. "The Cat and Fiddle" — a corruption of "Le Chat Fidèle" — is the highest public house in England; and the drive thither over the bare brown moors one Sunday afternoon under a lowering sky was dreary enough to make us hail with delight the sight of the stone image of a Cheshire cat that adorns the doorway. Chilled by the drive in the moorland wind, we crept into the shelter adjoining the public house for a cup of tea, and then had time for a brisk walk along the banks of a tiny rill to try in vain for the view of the Mersey that can be obtained from a certain point on a fine day. For the Cat and Fiddle is just within the boundaries of Cheshire, and it was by the way of Axe Edge, with a supposed view of Welsh mountains, that we returned in the teeth of a sharp shower over the bleak hills into Derbyshire.

A drive to Longnor recalled memories of Switzerland, for the rocky picturesqueness of the scenery has gained for the hamlet the name of Little Switzerland. The church here proved less interesting than we had supposed; but the farm-house, where we found the tea-table spread ready for our arrival, and the old spinet opened, and the chimney-piece garnished with flowers and bits of old china, and the solid mahogany chairs drawn around the table, recalled a chapter of George Eliot. It might have been the very house in

UNEXPECTED VISITORS.

Wirksworth, Derbyshire, which was the home of George Eliot's Aunt Samuel, the black-eyed, energetic little Methodist preacher who served as the model for the character of Dinah Morris in the story of "Adam Bede," and whose experience among condemned criminals furnished the motive of Hetty's life.

Along the Wye to Miller's Dale the Chee Tor is passed, — a straight, high rock towering above the road and connected with some story of a lover's leap; and a return on foot through the pine wood along the foot-path that follows the fringe of fern on the water's edge is to be recommended to every sojourner in Derbyshire. It is the custom on these drives to halt midway on the wide, open moor and pass a hat for the benefit of the guard and driver, — a sort of stand-and-deliver arrangement that no man can escape from; it is also cunningly arranged that just as you have driven far enough over the glorious, breezy moors with their wide horizon, to gain besides a delightful sense of freedom an acute appetite, the four horses are drawn up with a flourish before the inn, where the sumptuous afternoon tea in readiness seems a necessity, and the pennies and shillings and half-crown pieces follow one another out of sight with marvellous rapidity.

The excursion of all excursions in this neighborhood is the one that includes both Haddon Hall and Chatsworth, and fills the hours from eleven to six o'clock. Along the Wye and through and beyond the Miller's Dale, we sped one September morning, our way enlivened by song and anecdote; for there were musicians in our party, and a genial Roman Catholic priest was on the box-seat. At Rowsley, once called Rosely, from its abundance of roses, we stopped for a short time, then rattled on to Haddon Hall. Here the guard warned us that we must look lively and see we were all in the brake again in half an hour if we wished to see Chatsworth too. So with hurried steps we passed under the old stone gateway and through the Duke of Rutland's castle. Through the kitchen, offices, and chapel we went, where the priest showed us the traces of the altars built "before the Reformation, ladies," through the bedrooms, through the banqueting-hall, decorated everywhere with the family arms of the peacock and wild boar. Passing through the very door from which on the occasion of some festivity Dorothy Vernon escaped to elope with Sir John Manners (thus bringing the estate into the family of the Duke of Rutland), down the very stone steps her pretty feet trod into the terraced garden, we strolled for a little among the flower-beds, to look up at the vine-clad, battlemented walls and to wish that we had enough American dollars with us judiciously to restore the castle. One of the party, I know, was already

RURAL ENGLAND.

at work on a musical theme under the yew-trees, and another was meditating verses when the impatient guard sent us a message that we must be off.

An hour or so more brought us to Chatsworth, the property of the Duke of Devonshire. Lord Frederick Cavendish, the victim of the Phœnix Park murder, is buried in the churchyard in the village of Edensor, just at the gates of Chatsworth. Other members of the Cavendish family are buried in All Saints' Church in Derby, where there are monuments to their memory. Egeria went conscientiously over the palace and through the flower-gardens; but I contented myself with the view from the bridge of the exterior of the great building with its hundred gold-rimmed windows, and with a friend who felt likewise inclined, walked over to the inn at Edensor to order tea. So charmed were we with the inn and the lovely English landscape surrounding it, that we asked for the tariff, and seriously considered the prospect of a week at Edensor and an experience of fishing in the streams near by. When the party reassembled, it was found that the drowsy afternoon had given us a thirst like unto that of the old knights that visited Haddon Hall, where if a caitiff dared not empty at one draught the great flagon, he was chained by the wrist to the wall at a corner of the banqueting-room which the priest had pointed out to us, and the contents of the flagon were poured down his sleeve. Relays of many successive steaming teapots were needed before we were ready to respond to the guard's call, and take our places for the drive back to Buxton.

Through the Vale of the Dove we did not go, although it is noted for entrancing loveliness of scenery, nor did we visit the fishing-house on the banks of the Dove, which was built for Izaak Walton by his friend and disciple, Charles Cotton the poet. Beresford Hall, the home of the poet, was in the near neighborhood; and to entice the fisherman to fish and meditate near one who loved him, Charles Cotton

built the little fishing-house and placed on
the stone over the doorway the initial letters of their respective names, " twisted in
cipher," the date 1674, and the words " Pis-
catoribus Sacrum." Agreeably to Cotton's
request, a representation of this cipher was
put on the titlepage of his part of the
" Compleat Angler." The house stands
in an isolated position, sheltered by yew
and other trees, on a fine, smooth stream,
with a bowling-green, meadows, and mountains around it. In Izaak Walton's own
words, " The pleasantness of the river,
mountains, and meadows about it cannot
be described unless Sir Philip Sydney
or Mr. Cotton's father were again alive
to do it." Mr. Cotton expresses himself
thus in verse : —

> "My river still through the same channel glides,
> Clear from the tumult, salt, and dirt of tides,
> And my poor Fishing-House, my seat's best grace,
> Stands firm and faithful in the self-same place."

The Dove winds like a snake through the valley; and the deep, purling, clear waters of the Trent, the Wye, and the Derwent are equally well known among fishermen.

About half a mile from Eton College and within view of Windsor Castle may still be seen an eyot, where on a green lawn sloping down to the water's edge stands a modest fishing-house. Here, too, in the Thames, quietly, on a summer's evening, used Izaak Walton to sit "on a bank a-fishing" with the witty, cheerful, and learned provost of Eton, Sir Henry Wotton. On such a summer's evening, while reclining on the grasses on the brink of the river, did Sir Henry pencil the lines: —

> "Good Izaak, let us stay and rest us here;
>   Old friends when near
> Should talk together oft, and not lose time
>   In silly rhyme,
> That only addles men's good brains to write,
> While those who read bless God they don't indite.

"And I will not deny but I think myself a master in this." — IZAAK WALTON.

" There is a tree close by the river's side:
    There let 's abide,
And only hear far off the world's loud din,
    Where all is sin ;
While we our peaceful rods shall busy ply
When fish spring upward to the dancing fly."

www.ingramcontent.com/pod-product-compliance
Lightning Source LLC
Chambersburg PA
CBHW030754230426
43667CB00007B/959